101 Churches in Dorset

Jean Bellamy

Illustrations by
the late Eric Ricketts, R.I.B.A.

Photographs by the Author

S.B. Publications

BIBLIOGRAPHY

The Buildings of England: Dorset by John Newman and Nikolaus Pevsner (Penguin)
The King's England: Dorset by Arthur Mee (Hodder and Stoughton)
Highways and Byways in Dorset by Frederick Treves (re-issued Wildwood House)
A Shell guide - Dorset by Michael Pitt Rivers (Faber and Faber 1966)
Church Guides and Booklets

ACKNOWLEDGMENTS

I am indebted to the late Eric Ricketts R.I.B.A. for the first chapter, ARCHITECTURAL STYLE, and for all the pencil illustrations which make such a valuable contribution to this book. I would like to thank all those incumbents with whom I have been in touch, and to convey my apologies to those whom I have omitted to contact. I am indebted to the Rev. Robert H. G. Mason, Rector of Poole, for the picture postcard of St James's Church which he supplied; also to the Rev. Laurie Clow for the photograph of All Saints, Hampreston. The photograph of the Great West Window Sherborne Abbey, is included by kind permission of the Vicar and Churchwardens. would also like to thank Mr. E. Young, formerly organist of Steeple Church, for permission to use the postcard illustration of the Barrel Organ. Also to Andrew Stock for his painting of St. Hyppolytus Church and millennium gates, Ryme Intrinseca, and to the Vicar, The Rev. Philip J. Ringer, for supplying the picture. I am indebted to various church guides and leaflets.

By the same author
Treasures of Dorset (1991)
A Dorset Quiz Book (1995)
A Second Dorset Quiz Book (1997)

The Dorset Tea Trail (1999)
Dorset as She Wus Spoke (2002)
A Little Book of Dorset (2003)

First published in 2006 by S. B. Publications Tel: 01323 893498
Email: sbpublications@tiscali.co.uk

ISBN 1-85770-307-3

Designed and Typeset by EH Graphics (01273) 515527
Printed by Ethos Productions Ltd.

Front Cover: Abbotsbury, St Nicholas
Back Cover: Hermitage, St Mary

Preface

Visiting an old church can be a really fascinating experience from which a great deal can be learnt about the past. Most of us are aware of what a font or a pulpit looks like, but do we all know what a sanctuary ring is or a sedilia?

All old churches contain objects of interest and beauty many of which are described in the following pages. So as you explore these old buildings you should be able to identify them from the descriptions and illustrations given.

In medieval times churches were very ornate and colourful places, but there was a great deal of superstition and ignorance amongst the people. Only the priest was allowed to enter the sanctuary while the nave - which was often used for secular events – belonged to the people. Until the Reformation, services were spoken entirely in Latin which no one but the priest could understand. While the Mass was in progress, the congregation stood around in the nave (for there were no seats), chatted to friends and neighbours, bought and sold, begged for money, or did whatever took their fancy. The church had become very powerful and wealthy and the clergy slack and self-indulgent.

Then came John Wycliffe who lived from 1330-1384. He introduced the first complete translation of the Bible into English, so that everyone could understand it. Later William Tyndale (1492-1536), translated, printed and distributed the New Testament and Martin Luther (1483-1546), preached the doctrine of Justification by Faith. With the introduction of the first Prayer Book in Edward VI's reign, congregations were, for the first time, able to take part in worship. This was followed by Archbishop Cranmer's Prayer Book of 1552 which was finally revised in 1662. Today many churches use the more up-to-date service book known as Common Worship.

About 10,000 churches from medieval times exist in this country today, and almost every village possesses a church dating from Norman or even Saxon times. Old churches and the churchyards surrounding them are, in contrast to the noise and bustle of the world outside, peaceful places. So, as we explore them, it is worthwhile remembering that they are our heritage and responsibility, passed down to us by those who have gone before.

Contents

St. Georges Church.
Portland. Dorset.

Looking east.

This fine Classical Church
was designed in 1753.

The font.

Most of Wren's London
churches were built in
Portland stone, ferried
from the Island.

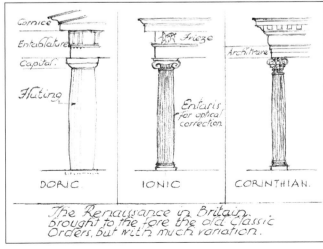

Cornice
Entablature
Capital.
Fluting

Frieze

Architrave

Entasis
for optical
correction

DORIC.   IONIC   CORINTHIAN.

The Renaissance in Britain
brought to the fore the old Classic
Orders, but with much variation.

1. Architectural Style

Architectural style varied over the centuries. The following table sets out the periods of architectural style which fall roughly into the following divisions:

AD 800-1100	Saxon	
1100-1200	Norman	- 12th century
1200-1300	Early English	- 13th century
1300-1400	Decorated	- 14th century
1400-1500	Perpendicular	- 15th century
1500-1600	Tudor	- 16th century

About the year 1600 AD, there came to our country a greater interest in the revival of the ancient styles of Greece and Rome. This period was called the Renaissance or Re-birth. St. Paul's Cathedral, London, is an example, but not the earliest. We can now put the Renaissance style into sub-divisions with approximate dates.

1600-1700	Jacobean	- 17th century

During this period, the emphasis was on the Classical or Greek/Roman styles.

1700-1800	Queen Anne and Georgian styles
1800-1850	Early 19th century, continuing the Classical styles.

THE 19TH CENTURY

From the middle of the 19th century, old styles of architecture were revived. As, for instance, the Houses of Parliament by Sir Charles Berry, built 1840 – 1860 in the 16th century Tudor style.

MODERN ARCHITECTURE

Few modern buildings are imitations of past styles, for costs, new materials, new ways of building, and new ideas must be allowed to flourish. We should not, however, forget our wonderful historical architectural heritage.

E. Ricketts, R.I.B.A.

2. In The Purbecks

WAREHAM, *Lady St. Mary*

Chapel of St Edward

The Parish church of Lady St. Mary is a fine building, its lofty tower a leading mark for shipping. It has a long history. The original church from Saxon times is thought to have been built on the site of what is now known as St. Edward's Chapel - at which time it would have been connected with the Nunnery of Ss. Mary, Peter and Ethelwold. It was probably twice destroyed during Danish raids on Wareham.

Edward the Martyr, murdered at Corfe Castle by his step-mother, Elfrida, is thought to have been buried on the east side of the present church, for a wooden building stood here until medieval times, possibly built over the site of the grave. During renovation of the church c1841, a coffin of Purbeck marble was, in fact, discovered under the floor of St. Edward's Chapel, believed to be the one in which the body of the young King was laid, until removal to Shaftesbury. This little medieval chapel with a Norman doorway is situated off the south side of the chancel, at a lower level, and for years was used as a coal cellar.

A striking feature of this church is the hexagonal lead font with figures of the twelve Apostles around the bowl. It is unique, being the only six-sided font in existence, and dates from c1100, the Purbeck stone base being about a century later. Two large Purbeck effigies date from the 13th century, and of particular interest are groups of old stones, two of them believed to have been supports of a Roman altar. Also surviving the rebuilding is the small Becket chapel over the sanctuary which has a sedilia and a double Norman piscina.

A former rector was John Hutchins, the Dorset historian (1743-73), the tablet to his memory having been put up by his son-in-law.

Hexagonal font

WAREHAM *St. Martin*

Situated near the northern rampart of the walls of Wareham, its nave tall and narrow in relation to its length, this little church (known as St. Martin's-on-the-Wall) is the best example of a Saxon church in Dorset. Some of it dates from c1030, and most of it from before 1100. It was restored and re-consecrated by W.H. Randall Blacking before the Second World War, after being found in a 'sad, dilapidated, reprehensibly neglected' state.

The north aisle was added in the 12th century and the tower, with its saddleback roof, in the 16th. The Saxon chancel arch has roll mouldings, and in the chancel and over the chancel arch are the remains of medieval, and older wall paintings from many centuries.

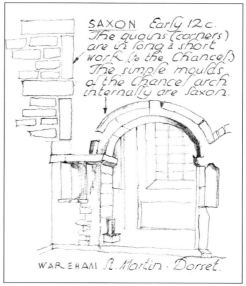

SAXON Early 12c.
The quoins (corners) are in long & short work (to the Chancel)
The simple moulds of the Chancel arch internally are Saxon.

WAREHAM *St. Martin · Dorset.*

St. Martin's is also noted for its memorial in the north aisle by Eric Kennington to that great personality, T.E. Lawrence, who died in 1935 and is buried at Moreton. The large marble effigy shows him lying at full length, clad in Arab robes and with his head resting on a camel saddle. By his side are the three books he always carried with him.

ARNE *St. Nicholas*

This small, well-buttressed 13th century church stands slightly elevated on the side of a hill in an isolated heathland setting famed for its wildlife, including rare birds, and – since the 1960s - an R.S.P.B. nature reserve. Worth visiting at all seasons of the year, this is a solitary, peaceful place where the heath runs down to the waters of Poole Harbour with its creeks and inlets, and one can follow a path down to the shore. The village derives its name from the Saxon aerne/aern, meaning 'a secret place'.

Built by monks in the 13th century, the little church is quite plain and possesses no division between chancel and nave. There is a 14th century font, and the original lancet windows survive. Over the door are the remains of wall-paintings.

Hanging on the wall beside the organ is the photograph of an elderly lady - a recent organist of the church for some twenty-five years, who died at the age of 96. She had been playing church organs since the age of 18.

To add to the church's charm, it is still lit by candlelight.

St Peter's

CHURCH KNOWLE, *St. Peter*

The village of Church Knowle lies about one mile westward from Corfe. The small ancient church of St. Peter is 13th century, though the tower was rebuilt in 1741. Its most striking feature is the threefold chancel arch, the centre arch of which is ancient though the side arches are more modern. There is a 13th century window in the chancel with little figures of Luke and Peter, put there in 1930 by children in memory of their parents.

The list of rectors dates back to 1327 and the church registers, now lodged with the Dorset County Archivist at Dorchester, go back to 1548. They contain records of those who, in order to stimulate the woollen industry, were buried in wool between the years 1685 and 1789, this strange custom being compulsory for a period of one hundred and twenty years.

In the church lies John Clavell whose family came to England with the Conqueror. He ordered his elaborate tomb to be made in 1572, though he did not die until forty years later. In the churchyard a tombstone shows a man in modern dress feeding birds and squirrels, his epitaph stating that he was one of those merciful folk who will obtain mercy. The graves above slope towards the hills in which skeletons of ancient inhabitants of Dorset lie in hollows cut in the chalk.

STEEPLE *St. Michael*

Here is a 15th century church with restorations, standing on a small hill in a woodland setting (churches dedicated to St. Michael were often situated on a hill), along with just two houses. The rectory is Tudor in design; the church has a Norman south doorway.

The lords of the manor of Steeple were the Lawrences, one branch of the family being the Washingtons, from which line George Washington was descended. Over Steeple's church porch may be seen the coat of arms, cut in stone, of the Lawrence family. It contains an emblem of six stars and six stripes, and is repeated in scarlet paint on the barrel roof of the church.

1858 Barrel Organ

Inside the building is a barrel organ which perhaps was known to Thomas Hardy, one of whose string-playing characters in one of his books refers to these instruments as 'miserable dumbledores'. There are not many barrel

organs in existence today, the pipe-work of most having been incorporated into the traditional-type organ. The barrel organ at Steeple has been very skilfully restored in recent years and now stands in the north transept of the little church. In regular use until about 1910, it probably remained playable until, due to deterioration as a result of non-use, it was dismantled in 1943. Until restoration in 1990 it had been on display in the vestry. It has three barrels each containing twelve tunes.

Steeple (Purbecks)

KINGSTON *St. James*

This village, situated 400ft. high on a hilltop, commands extensive views towards Corfe Castle. It possesses two churches, the older – small and now disused - was built c1838 by John Scott, first Earl of Eldon and Lord Chancellor of England. In the churchyard are buried Lord Eldon and his wife.

By way of contrast, the other and more recent is by G.E. Street and dates from c1875 - a fine Gothic Revival church, vaulted in stone and possessing a tall, massive central tower which seems to dominate what is a

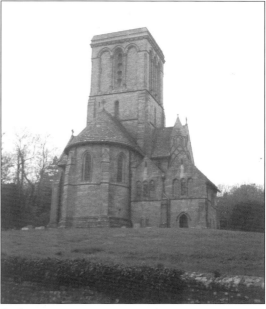

St James

comparatively small church and is a local landmark. Built internally of local Purbeck stone quarried from Lord Eldon's estate, chancel and transepts have stone-groined roofs, and there is a sedilia and piscina also of local marble. There is a fine wrought iron screen and a wrought iron pulpit with a marble pedestal, and some good stained glass in the windows by Clayton and Bell. Access is by way of a western narthex.

This church has been described as being 'like a miniature Early English cathedral built all of a piece'.

STUDLAND *St. Nicholas*

(Patron Saint of sailors, travellers and children).

This lovely little, almost entirely Norman, church (of which it is the best example in Dorset, and one of the oldest and best-preserved of its kind in the country) is of Saxon origin reconstructed in the 12th century. It has a squat tower, buttressed in the 13th

St Nicholas

century and covered with lichen, blood-red in parts, which remained unfinished due to the danger of settlement. There is a room or loft in the upper storey of the tower, said to have been a priest's chamber. It is approached by a small door high up on the outside of the tower.

The Chancel

The chancel is dimly-lit in spite of window enlargement in the 17th century, and appears almost to be enclosed by its moulded Norman arches and carved capital vaulting. Above it may be seen the remains of a 15th century printed text. The east window is Early English.

In the nave are quaint, well-preserved roof corbels. Some of the Norman windows remain though most have been enlarged by 18th century builders. The font is plain and Norman, the pulpit 18th century. There is a Norman south door, and there are a number of hatchments, and traces of wall-paintings.

Outside, a consecration cross may be seen at the north-east corner of the church. At the rear, the churchyard slopes down towards the church, with views of the cliffs to Ballard Down. There are several very old yew trees.

Visited at Christmas time as dusk was approaching, this ancient church, lit only in the chancel, held a magical quality.

The Last Supper

WORTH MATRAVERS *St. Nicholas*

This attractive Purbeck village possesses a Norman church – one of the oldest in Dorset - with traces of Saxon origin, reminiscent of Studland church, though it lacks its mystery. It stands on a hillside with extensive views of the English Channel, and consists of nave (c1150), chancel and west tower built later in the same century - though the stone pyramidal roof was part of the 1869 restoration. There is a Saxon doorway blocked up within its 12th century walls, and over the south door is a badly worn Norman tympanum.

The interior has a very fine, massive Norman chancel arch with chevron ornament, resting on six piers with carved capitals. Behind it is a 14th century east window. Corbel tables exist around the eaves of nave and chancel. The windows are mostly small and high in the walls for, as Arthur Mee points out, being only one mile from the cliff, the villagers were in danger from sea raids and the church would have been their refuge.

In the graveyard, amongst some old coffin lids carved with crosses, is the burial place of a famous son of the village, Benjamin Jesty and his wife, the inscription on the stone reading, 'An upright and honest man, particularly noted for having been the first person (known) that introduced the Cow Pox by inoculation, and who from his great strength of mind, made the experiment from the cow on his wife and two sons in the year 1774'.

Remote in its situation near the cliff top on St. Aldhelm's Head and in the same parish is St. Aldhelm's Chapel – a strange building, 32ft. square with a pyramidal stone roof crowned with a cross, having neither tower nor porch. Its walls are thick and buttressed and it is undoubtedly Norman. Within its bare dark interior, internal cross-vaulting is supported by a massive central pillar. The little building was at one time known as the Devil's Chapel but has since been re-consecrated.

3. In The Churchyard

Before going into the church pause and take a look around the churchyard. These are usually peaceful places, well named 'God's Acre', and are often natural havens for wildlife, attracting a wide variety of flora and fauna. A number of churchyards in West Dorset, including Abbotsbury, Broadmayne, Whitchurch Canonicorum and Netherbury have been awarded certificates of merit under a project run by the Dorset Wildlife Trust.

Gargoyle Look up towards the church roof and you may see a number of weird, grotesquely carved faces on the corners and sides of the tower, or on the upper parts of the walls. These are *gargoyles* and they probably date from between the 12th and 16th centuries. Our ancestors were very fond of decorating their churches in this way, for they believed them to be full of dragons and demons from which the gargoyles would protect them.

Gargoyle

Our ancestors obviously had a sense of humour too. Sometimes one comes across a gargoyle with its hand in its mouth, or in the wide-open mouth of another, or a water-spouting gargoyle. The word 'gargoyle' comes from a French word meaning 'throat', the water-spout projecting from the mouth serving the useful purpose of throwing rainwater from the roof clear of the walls of the church.

Graves and Gravestones Many graveyards possess ancient *graves* and *gravestones*, some of which may date back to the 1700s or even 1600s. Often the lettering on these old tombs is difficult to read, having been eroded away over the years or covered with lichen. Graveyards are particularly popular with folk tracing their family trees, for useful information on one's ancestors can be discovered from gravestones. Members of family history societies often spend time carefully recording the information on all the headstones in a particular graveyard for the benefit of other members of the society.

The oldest graves lie mostly to the south of the church, the north side - with the shadow of the church falling on it - was believed to be the meeting place of evil spirits.

Dole table

Table Tomb and Dole Table Flat-topped, rectangular tombs resembling tables are – not surprisingly – known as *table-tombs* and they are often very ancient. A table-top tomb standing close to the main door of the church could be a *dole-table* for it was the custom for wealthy people to give money to provide a 'dole' of bread for the poor, and this was distributed from the dole table. Those receiving the dole were expected to attend the church, and the bread - which was given to them after the service - was kept in a 'dole cupboard' until needed. (see chap. 12 Powerstock)

Church Door The main door into the church may be massive, unlocked by an enormous key. Ancient doors exist, even from the 13th century, some still hanging on their original hinges and opened by means of their original iron ring. One such is in the Norman north doorway of the parish church of St.Mary, Maiden Newton (see chap.16).

Ancient door

There was a strange belief existing well into the 20th century that to enter a church by the west door (which was never used except to bear out the coffin at funerals), foreshadowed untimely death. Another curious belief was that the devil entered the church by the north door and perhaps this is the reason for the *blocked-up doorways* which are sometimes to be seen in the north walls of churches.

Doorway If the church doorway is high and narrow with a round arch, then it is probably Anglo-Saxon; if rounded and heavily ornamented or having a number of rounded arches one inside the other, then it is probably Norman.

Tympanum A recessed space beneath an arch of a doorway, triangular or semi-circular in shape and ornamented, is known as a *tympanum*. The Normans sometimes filled in the head of a doorway in this manner. (see chap. 16 Wynford Eagle)

Yew Tree Often to be found in churchyards are *yew trees*, sometimes taller than the church itself, and believed by some to be the remains of the groves in which pagan worship took place. Being evergreen and with their gnarled and twisted trunks, they were looked upon as symbols of immortality, noted for their longevity. Some say that yew trees were planted in churchyards rather than in fields because their leaves are poisonous to cattle, though it was to protect the church from storm and rain that King Edward I ordered them to be so planted. Others say that they were planted to supply bows for the archers. Two rows of six yew trees on either side of the pathway from the church gate to the front entrance are said to represent the twelve Apostles.

Should there be six yew trees on one side of the path, five on the other, with a twelfth standing slightly apart from the rest, the latter is believed to represent Judas Iscariot.

Lych-gate Sometimes the entrance to the churchyard forms a *lych-gate*, beneath which there may be a raised oblong block, either of wood or stone in the centre. In times past, the priest would conduct part of the burial service from the lych-gate, with the coffin resting on the block. Stone benches on either side of the block were intended for the priest to rest upon while he awaited the arrival of the coffin. Lych-gates are also known as *'Corpse-Gates'*, *'lych'* being the old English word for a dead body. (see chap. 8 Hazelbury Bryan)

Lych-gate

Coffin In medieval times, only the wealthy were given the luxury of a coffin which did not come into general use until the end of the 17th century. The poor were brought to their funeral in a parish coffin, out of which the body would be taken and wrapped in a sheet for burial. In 1678, in order to boost the wool trade, an Act of Parliament was passed forbidding anyone to be buried unless wrapped in woollen material. The penalty for not complying was a fine of £5. The Act was repealed in 1814. (chap. 2 Church Knowle)

Preaching Cross There may be a *preaching cross* in the churchyard. Preaching crosses are quite large and consist of a shaft topped by a cross with a flight of steps around the base, though sometimes the cross is missing. As the name suggests, they were used in olden times as positions from which to preach. (see chap. 16 Cheselbourne)

Preaching cross

Stocks Seen occasionally are *stocks*, either in the churchyard or inside the church. In past times, petty thieves and others were punished by being forced to

sit with their legs locked in the stocks, exposed to taunts and beatings and other indignities such as being pelted with rotten eggs. (The pillory served the same purpose, with the wrongdoer being made to stand on a raised platform with head and arms through the holes in the crosspiece). (see chap. 10 Holnest)

Stocks

Mounting-block Rarer still is the *mounting-block* by the churchyard wall. In days gone by folk rode to church by horse-back or walked - there were no cars! So mounting-blocks were provided for their use.

Sanctuary Ring Even rarer are *sanctuary rings* which are more often to be found on the main doors of cathedrals, Durham being an example. In times past, anyone wishing to escape from the clutches of the law had only to hold onto the sanctuary ring to obtain protection from arrest. At one time every church and churchyard was a sanctuary for criminals, and if a person who had committed a crime could reach such sanctuary before being waylaid and arrested he would be safe. For once within the sanctuary, if he confessed within forty days and took a solemn oath before the coroner to leave the country and never return, he would be allowed to go free. (see chap.16 Puddletown)

Statue Niches Empty *statue niches* may sometimes be seen on the outside walls of churches. These may or may not have contained statues of saints before the Reformation.

Priest's Door Occasionally there is a small blocked-up door (known as a *priest's door*) leading from the churchyard into the church by way of the chancel (see chap. 7).

Buttress The buttress was a construction, usually of brick or stone, built to support the roof or walls of a building – though sometimes it was added merely for ornamental purposes. It is sometimes called a 'pier'.

Epitaph Before leaving the churchyard, take another look at the gravestones to see if there are any interesting, unusual or amusing *epitaphs*. (There may be gravestones inside the church too). Here are some examples:

In the churchyard at Steepleton is to be seen the following epitaph to the village idiot, Jack Webber, harmless and loved by everyone. It was written by the squire, who thought him to be wise at last:

'Near this stone Jack Webber lies,
As Croesus rich, as Solomon wise'.

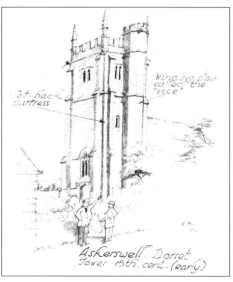

Askerswell, Dorset
Tower 15th. cent. (early)

The Squire himself died in 1811 and wrote his own epitaph:

'We die and are forgotten; 'tis heaven's decree;
Thus the fate of others will be the fate of me'.

At the east end of Melbury Bubb churchyard lies Richard Handleigh, rector of the church for 59 years, from 1587 - 1646. His epitaph reads as follows:

'A withered Hand leigh here do I
By sin with death oppressed
God's mighty hand shall raise me up
By faith in Christ to rest'.

A rather picturesque idea is the placing of sheep in country churchyards for the purpose of keeping the grass down.

4. Blandford / Wimborne Area

WIMBORNE MINSTER *St. Cuthberga*

Wimborne's most notable feature is its squat two-towered Minster which was formerly a collegiate church but is now parochial. It presents a curiously mottled appearance, being built of at least two types of stone varying from red to pale grey. The central tower (84ft.) had a spire which collapsed circa 1600; the 15th century bell-tower rises 95ft. from the street. The main fabric of the Minster is Norman, the nave arcades with their pointed arches dating from this period. The choir stalls are Jacobean of 1610, the reading desk and choir-stalls of the early 17th century, and there is 15th century Flemish glass. Amongst the Minster's other treasures

Three faced sundial

are the Beaufort tomb (15th century), and a chained library of 1686. High up on the south wall of the west tower is the Astronomical Clock, built by a monk of Glastonbury in 1320, its mechanism is operated by enormous weights.

Another feature of the Minster is the Ettricke tomb, otherwise known as the 'Man in the Wall'. Ettricke, a recorder of Poole, claimed to have been offended by the people of Wimborne and said he would neither be buried in the church or outside it, nor yet in the ground or above it. He afterwards had second thoughts and whilst wishing to be buried in the Minster, did not wish to break his vow. So he was granted permission to be buried within a niche in the wall and had his coffin prepared in readiness for his death. He had been convinced that this would take place in 1691, but in the event it did not occur until 1703, and the alteration in the date is clearly visible.

A very popular figure in the town is the Quarter Jack, situated on the outside of the west tower. He dates from 1613 and started life as a monk - though since Napoleon's time he has been a brightly-painted Grenadier. Four times every hour he carries out his routine of striking the quarter. The two leather buckets on either side of him were at one time part of the fire-fighting equipment of the town.

Outside near the south porch is a very large, three-faced sundial.

TARRANT CRAWFORD *St. Mary*

This small church, originally dedicated to All Saints, stands near the site of a former Cistercian abbey. It dates from the 12th/13th centuries, though worship here probably goes even farther back in time. It has a Norman chancel and a 13th century nave. The tower was added in the early 16th century.

Said to be one of the most interesting churches in the diocese, its most remarkable feature is the series of 14th century wall-paintings which cover most of the nave and which were partially revealed during restoration work in 1910-11. Further exposed and treated in 1948, those on the upper part of the south wall are believed to be the most extensive and complete of any frescoes in the country. In fourteen scenes they depict the story of St. Margaret of Antioch's refusal to marry the Provost Olybrius, her imprisonment, and the lurid punishments subsequently meted out to her.

Here, too, is a Jacobean font and there are fragments of stained glass in the 15th century nave window. There are three bells of which two are medieval. In the chancel is a 12th century pillar bowl (piscina), and a blocked-up priest's door. The restoration work of 1911 included re-arrangement of the old box pews, parts of which were used to provide the panelling at the east end, and in the construction of new pews. A coffin lid with a foliated cross originally came from the site of the Abbey church and is pointed out as being that of Bishop Poore, who partially built and later became Bishop of Salisbury Cathedral (1217), and afterwards of Durham (1228). At the end of his life he expressed a wish to be buried in the abbey.

Another coffin lid is said to be that of Queen Joan, daughter of King John and wife of King Alexander of Scotland. She, too, was devoted to the Abbey (which had existed at Tarrant Crawford from 1223), and requested that she should be laid to rest there. Both tombs, which were formerly situated in the Abbey chapel, have long since perished.

The village of Tarrant Crawford lies half-a-mile from the church and is

largely deserted. It is believed to have been moved to achieve isolation for the abbey. Of the latter a barn and possibly part of an adjoining farmhouse survive. This church is now in the care of The Churches Conservation Trust. A service of Holy Communion is held here at 10.30am on the fourth Sunday of every month from May to September.

Tarrant Crawford

TARRANT RUSHTON *St. Mary*

Tarrant Rushton

This small attractive 12th century church with Norman tower - said to be one of the most remarkable in Dorset – stands across the stream from the valley road. Multi-coloured, in brown and grey stone and flint both inside and out, it is constructed in the shape of a Greek cross, all four arms being equal in length. The chancel arch dates back to c1150, and one of the transepts is 13th century, while the other has a 15th century window with a mass dial below. It was restored in the 1870s and again in 1963. New oak furniture was introduced some forty years ago.

Of particular interest is the window tracery in the squint, two hagioscopes thought to be 600 years old, and some medieval fragments set in the fabric after restoration work. In the west wall of the transept is a leper window, legend having it that marks in the stonework outside were caused by lepers pressing against it to see into the church. These appear to have been made by inmates of the nearby leper hospital of St. Leonard.

Inside, over the doorway, is a marble lintel inscribed with two figures, one holding a book and the other a dove, while between them is a 12th century carving of a lamb bearing a cross and scroll. They are thought to represent the Trinity.

Other features to look out for include two piscinas, and two round earthenware pots built into the eastern face of the chancel arch. The latter are believed to be amplifiers (acoustic jars) from medieval times, placed there in 1458 to enhance the priest's voice.

During the Second World War, the downs above the village became the site of an airfield, later to become the base for experiments carried out by Sir Alan Cobham's Flight Refuelling Company. Sir Alan and Lady Cobham are buried in the churchyard.

TARRANT HINTON St. Mary

Tarrant Hinton

Of mainly 13th and 15th century origin, this unspoiled church originally belonged to Shaftesbury Abbey. It stands back from the road in an attractive setting and has some large ancient stone gargoyles and battlements on its fine stone tower – the latter having been started in the time of John de Tarent, the earliest rector of the church. It is thought that an earlier church once existed on the site, there being fragments of Norman carving incorporated into the outside wall above the porch door.

The exterior is mainly constructed of alternate bands of flint and green sandstone, this being typical of this part of Dorset. The interior, with its unplastered flint walls, contains a chapel of the 15th century on the north side of the chancel, with decorated Renaissance arches. The south aisle is also of the 15th century, though the chancel was rebuilt in 1874 at the time of the church's restoration by Benjamin Ferrey.

Of particular interest is the Purbeck marble Norman font with a 17th century oak cover, the late 17th century Communion rails of carved oak from Pembroke College, Cambridge, and an Art Nouveau wrought-iron lectern of 1909. On the south side of the chancel is a hagioscope with glass, though the most notable feature is an Easter Sepulchre of the early 16th century in the north wall, with carved angels above its canopied recess. It bears the initials TW, being those of the rector from 1514 to 1536, and the Latin inscription is taken from St. Matthew chapter 28 verse 6 - *'Come and see the place where the Lord was laid'*.

High on the north wall of the nave is the coat of arms of George III, and nearby is a bronze plaque bearing the inscription, 'Michael Hankey, Fighter Pilot Fleet Air Arm - killed in combat over Malta 12th August 1942'. In the south aisle, is a Norman piscina, its position showing that an altar once

Interior

existed here. Farther along to the right is the Millennium Window based on Joel 2, vv. 21-27.

Tarrant Hinton lies four miles north-east of Blandford. It is one of ten parishes making up the Chase benefice.

BLANDFORD FORUM *Ss. Peter and Paul*

Rebuilt in Classical style of Greensand ashlar by the Bastard Brothers after the fire of 1731 which destroyed most of the town, this church has a west tower with a balustraded parapet and timber bell turret. There is an original west gallery, font and pulpit, along with low box pews and a mayor's seat. The chancel was lengthened in the 19th century in matching style, the original apsidal sanctuary being reconstructed at this time.

On the night of the fire the church was saved until about 11 pm, but the defenders were by that time too tired to continue and sadly the building was left to burn down.

Prominent on the pavement in front of the church is a Doric portico of 1760, built by John Bastard to house a pump, as a commemoration of the fire and as a safeguard against future calamities.

Doric portico

SPETISBURY *St. John the Baptist*

Spetisbury church

The church is a low building of brown stone and flint, rebuilt in 1859 by T.H. Wyatt, though the massive Norman tower, also multi-coloured and believed to date from c1350, remains unaltered. It has a cradle roof with ribs and fine bosses, and features of interest include a font of Purbeck marble, probably of the same age as the tower. Chained to the lectern is a 300 year-old copy of Bishop Jewel's famous *Apology* which in 1610 was ordered to be placed in every parish church.

A fine canopied tomb of 1599 is a memorial to one John Bowyer, Lord of the Manor of Spetisbury, while a brass commemorates Stephen Groves, notable organist of the church for over 50 years until his death in 1907. The pulpit is Jacobean and beautifully carved, but a preaching hour-glass set in an iron frame of 1700 and formerly affixed to the wall behind it disappeared some years ago.

In the churchyard is a modern-looking pyramid grave commemorating a 19th century former rector, Thomas Rackett, and his family. The list of incumbents on the north-east pillar of the tower reveals him to have been in office for 60 years from 1780 to 1840, rendering him the longest-serving rector. He had wide interests, including music, painting, poetry, natural history, architecture and archaeology, and some of his collection of ancient seals and coins are in Dorset County Museum, along with a number of bundles of correspondence and written notes. His various extra-parochial activities led to a charge of neglecting his parish, though he was apparently able to vindicate himself.

Another rector, and the most well-known, was Charles Sloper who held office from 1705 to 1727. The parsonage house in which he lived is now called John's House, and in the basement of this once medieval building, rebuilt by him in 1716, are walls of clay said to date from c1200. The present rectory, built in 1954, stands near to John's House.

It is recorded that in 1348-49 during the Black Death, Spetisbury lost two of its rectors as well as two vicars. For as long as records exist this church has formed one ecclesiastical parish with Charlton Marshall.

WINTERBORNE TOMSON *St. Andrew*

Winterborne Tomson

This is one of the Blandford Winterborne villages, access to which is via the Wimborne to Dorchester road, taking the Winterborne Kingston turning beyond Winterborne Zelstone. The atmospheric, well-kept little Norman church (said to be one the most interesting of the Winterbornes) has a squat wooden bell turret and stands close to a farmyard. Deserted and disused for many years, dusty and moth-eaten, it was restored c1931 by A.R. Powys (for 25 years secretary of the Society for Protection of Ancient Buildings) who lies buried in the churchyard, along with his wife, Faith. Some documents on architecture by Thomas Hardy were sold to provide funds, and a notice states that 'St. Andrew's was restored by the Redundant Churches Fund of St. Andrew by the Wardrobe, London'. The church is now in the care of The Churches Conservation Trust (formerly the Redundant Churches Fund).

The east end is apsidal and there is a plastered wagon roof with carved bosses. The interior has altered little since it was refurnished in the early 18th century. There is a 15th century font, simple screen, west gallery, and Communion rails. Of particular interest are the plain pine box pews and the two-decker pulpit with sounding board.

Winterborne Tomson gets is name from an owner of land called Thomas. In 1242 it was known as Winterborne Thom.

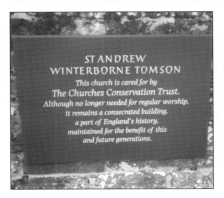

Interior showing box pews

WINTERBORNE ZELSTONE *St. Mary*

Winterborne Zelstone

Rebuilt in 1865, but retaining its 15th century tower, this charming little church of banded flint and heathstone is situated in a peaceful village of thatched cottages and modern houses. It has a low tower with Portland stone crenellations, and a gargoyle in the form of an ox's head. There is a small turret staircase on the west side.

The light, airy interior, which has a 15th century tower window, was restored by Digby Wyatt in 1866. A wooden plaque dated 1957 states that the lighting was given in memory of the Barrett family, and there is mention of an unknown benefactor who many years ago gave a field for the maintenance of the church. The organ was given to the church by the Royal Corps of Signals, who kept it in repair.

On the river bank nearby stands a medieval stone cross, re-erected to commemorate the Silver Jubilee of Queen Elizabeth in 1977. The name of the village means 'estate on the river Winterborne held by the de Seles family who came from Zeals in Wiltshire'.

Interior

5. Inside the Church

Porch As we enter the main entrance of the church we find ourselves in the porch. This is usually situated on the south side of the church though sometimes on the north side if there is - or was - a manor house there. There were few porches in the 12th and 13th centuries, though they increased in the 14th century.

Today porches are merely places through which one passes to enter the main part of the church, though

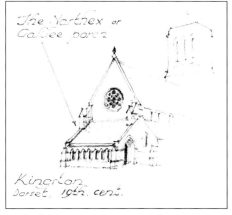

The Narthex or Galilee porch

Kington
Dorset. 19th. cent.

from the 14th century onwards they had different uses. Baptisms used to take place in the porch, also the reading of marriage banns, and even parts of the marriage service. Coroner's courts were held in the porch too, executors of wills paid out legacies, and other business was transacted. There were usually stone or wooden seats on each side.

Two-storey porch In medieval times, porches sometimes had rooms built over them which were used to store the parish armour, or as a library or meeting place, or to house church books and documents. Sometimes they served as an early type of school where boys were taught Latin.

Narthex This is the name given to an enclosed vestibule or covered porch (also called a 'Galilee') at the main entrance to a church. The name is 17th century and comes via Latin from Medieval Greek. The word means 'giant fennel', the stems of which were used to make boxes - and so it came to mean an enclosure or enclosed porch. In the early Christian church, the narthex was used for the instruction of catechumens (those receiving instruction prior to baptism), who were not allowed to enter the church itself until they had been baptised.

Nave The *nave* is the name given to the main body of the church. The word comes from the latin '*Navis*' - a ship. Saxon churches were built with a chancel to shelter the altar, and the people built their own shelter – the nave. The two joined together formed the early church plan as we know it today. The Normans added an aisle and transepts which gave the cross formation of today.

Font The *font* is usually to be found close to the main door (or it may be midway between north and south of the west end) for, as we have already seen, baptisms began in the porch, or even outside the main door, and finished at the font which needed to be near at hand.

If the font is square in shape and supported by four pillars at the corner, it is probably *Norman*. There are a great many Norman fonts in existence today and sometimes they are the oldest feature in the church for the font may have been retained even when the church was rebuilt.

Stone tubs without decoration may be Saxon or early Norman. Sometimes the bowl (or rounded part) is older than the base on which it stands, the

Hexagonal font

reason being that in Saxon times it was the custom for adults to be baptised by having water poured over them though later it was mainly children who were baptised. This was done by immersion (being submerged) so fonts were raised on low stands. Later still, when sprinkling became popular, the font bases became higher and the bowl smaller.

Many fonts are octagonal (eight-sided) in shape, eight being the number of resurrection and new life. In the church of Lady St. Mary, Wareham (see chap. 2), exists a unique hexagonal (six-sided) 12th century lead font with figures of the twelve apostles.

Font Cover Originally fonts did not have covers, but later they were given flat ones which were kept locked. This was because of a superstitious belief that the holy water kept inside the font possessed magical powers and sometimes people would try to steal it.

In the 15th century very tall elaborately carved *font covers* came into being. Being very heavy they were raised by means of a pulley - either rope or chain. There are still some of these tall font covers in existence, though not very many. (chap. 16 Cattistock)

Belfry Towards the back (west end) of the church lies the *belfry*, the part of the tower in which the bells are hung. As bells are weighty, the tower needs to be strong. Sometimes the belfry was reached by means of a *staircase-turret* in the tower, by stairs built into the thickness of the wall, or by a thick wooden ladder. If the ladder was not a fixture, it could be drawn up into the belfry - an advantage in times of war and hostile attacks upon the church.

Gallery A gallery at the west end of the church may be a musicians' (or minstrels') gallery. (see chap. 17 Stinsford).

Before the Reformation there would have been an organ in most churches and it would have been situated in the rood loft – hence 'organ loft'. (see chapter 7). During Oliver Cromwell's time, however, (known as 'the Commonwealth'), the use of organs in churches was forbidden and many were destroyed – so that by the time of 'the Restoration', when Charles II came to the throne, there were no organs to accompany the singing. As a result groups of musicians banded together and played simple musical instruments which included the pitch-pipe, trumpet, bassoon, flute, clarinet, hautboy, bass-fiddle, and violoncello. Minstrels' galleries were provided for their use, sometimes built from parts of rood screens which had been taken down (see chapter 7). During the singing of hymns the congregation would turn to face the gallery. (see chap. 17 Stinsford). Some musical instruments still survive.

With the restoration of organs in the 18th century, however, and the siting of surpliced choirs of men and boys in the chancel, minstrels' galleries were no longer needed so they were used as extra seating for the congregations which were large in those days.

A composite sketch of the Music Gallery, Stinsford, Dorset, circa 1860

from a Gallery plan by Thomas Hardy.

6. Cranborne / Wimborne Area

CRANBORNE Ss. Mary, Peter, and Bartholomew

Ss Mary, Peter and Bartholomew

This fairly large church adjoins the site of a Benedictine Priory (where was once a Saxon church) and has a Norman doorway. It dates mainly from 1252 when it was rebuilt in Early English style. A substantial tower of 1440 was presented by Richard Duke of Gloucester and his wife, Anna, their arms appearing on two shields on either side of the west door. The chancel was rebuilt in the 19th century, and the nave has a barrel roof.

There is a finely carved pulpit of oak dating from cl400 and bearing the initials 'T.P.', probably those of Thomas Parker, Abbot of Tewkesbury who died in 1421.

Amongst a number of good monuments are the Stillingfleet memorials, Edward Stillingfleet, Bishop of Worcester, born 1635, being noted for his acts of charity. There is also one to John Elliot, depicting a youth sitting in a recess with his head propped on one hand and a skull on his knee. Said to be a clever child, he died suddenly in 1641 at the age of seven. A window of date 1885 is to John Tregonwell who became the founder of the town of Bournemouth.

Also to be seen are 14th century wall-paintings of St. Christopher carrying the child Jesus and being bitten by a fish, a Christ in Majesty, and a Tree of the Seven Deadly Sins. There is also a royal arms of 1709.

Once an important market town, Cranborne was at one time the centre of the Cranborne Chase Court.

WIMBORNE ST. GILES

Standing adjacent to a row of attractive almshouses of 1624, this Georgian church, said to have been built in 1514 by Sir Anthony Ashley, was rebuilt in 1732 in Classical style. It has a balustraded tower and walls of flint and stone.

Wimborne St Giles

Redecorated in the 19th century by G.F. Bodley in Gothic style, much of his work was destroyed by a fire in 1908, following which it was remodelled by Sir Ninian Comper, who brought back the church's Classical character. A south aisle was created and a north aisle added, and with one broad aisle the interior is almost square. Most of the fittings are by Comper, including the font cover, the rood screen at the east end, and a gallery at the west, the latter supporting the organ – all in Gothic style. The font, which survived the fire, is of the 18th century, and there is an 18th century Royal Arms.

The church has many memorials to the Ashley Coopers, St. Giles House being the seat of the Earls of Shaftesbury. There is a canopied monument to Sir Anthony Ashley who built the almshouses, and is reputed to have introduced the cabbage to this country. The lst, 4th and 7th Earls are commemorated, the latter being one of the great Parliamentarians of the Victoria era – a great reformer who did so much to fight wrong and injustice wherever he saw it.

GUSSAGE *All Saints, St. Michael and St. Andrew*

All Saints

The three Gussage churches stand in an open chalk valley of Cranborne Chase, near the old Roman road, Ackling Dyke. A brook, (which joins up with the river Allen), runs through the villages and gives them their name. Gussage All Saints and Gussage St. Michael stand south of the A354, while Gussage St. Andrew is the other side of the main Blandford to Salisbury road.

All Saints, the largest, is a beautiful little building, its tall, flint-banded 14th century tower topped by pinnacles of the 15th century. Restored in 1865, it is mostly new but possesses three pre-Reformation bells. The font is Norman, and the 18th century mahogany-cased organ originally came from Westminster Abbey. Its registers date from 1560. The ancient name of Gussage All Saints was Gussage Regis, an indication that it belonged to the Crown until given to the nunnery of Tarent.

Gussage St. Michael, mentioned in the Domesday Book, has a church of flint and stone with six roof levels. It possesses fine old bells in its tower, the latter begun by the Normans and completed c1350. Two of the bells, cast in the year Elizabeth I died, have inscriptions 'Feare God' and 'Hope well'. A medieval wooden ladder staircase leads to the belfry, and there is a colourful Victorian reredos, a rood screen dating from 1895, and a Caroline Royal Arms. The font is 700 years old, and there is a clerestory going back 500 years and a 300 year-old oak roof. In the churchyard is a magnificent yew tree, 15ft. in girth.

Gussage St. Andrew has a small flint 12th century church standing at the top of a farmyard. Generally known as Minchington, it is noted for its 13th and 14th century frescoes which have recently been restored. There are 13th century lancet windows, the roof over the nave is 15th century, and there is a 17th century pulpit. Although heated by electricity, the little building is illuminated by candlelight, giving it a simple charm.

The name 'Minchington' is derived from the old Anglo-Saxon word for a nun – 'Myncheon'. A small wooden chapel was erected here but was destroyed by fire c1250, to be later replaced by the present church.

KNOWLTON

Knowlton Church

The ruins of Knowlton church stand approximately 300 yards from its deserted medieval village and date from the 12th century. It is a small church even though considerably enlarged in the 15th century, at which time there could have been an increase in population. Its eventual depopulation was, it is thought, a result of the plague. At one time a chapel-of-ease to Horton, it fell into disrepair c1650 and remained unused for many years. Early in the 18th century, somewhere around the year 1735, it was repaired, but unfortunately the roof fell in soon afterwards and it was never used again.

The ruins stand within a circular earthwork with two entrances. Unlike most parish churches, the siting of Knowlton church may have had other, more mysterious reasons – possibly deliberately erected to Christianise a pagan shrine. It is probable that this site (like other similar sites) was of religious significance for thousands of years, even though the church itself was not built until the 11th or 12th century.

Be this as it may, worship continued at Knowlton from about 1800 BC until the church was abandoned in comparatively recent times, evidence for the existence of this continuity of worship being stronger here than anywhere else in Dorset.

The surrounding sward is well-kept. The masonry of the church is of flint and dark red sandstone, with limestone corner-stones and arches, similar to many other east Dorset churches. The surviving tower is 15th century and the windows Early English, whilst the nave and chancel are Norman.

The encircling earthwork, a bank with a ditch, is approximately 100 yards across, and is a prehistoric 'henge' or ritual monument of the Bronze Age (c1800 BC), the purpose of which was to protect the outside world from the egress of malignant spirits confined within the church.

KNOWLTON CHURCH
AND EARTHWORKS

AN EARLY NORMAN CHURCH REMODELLED IN THE 14TH CENTURY AND STANDING ON THE CENTRAL PLATEAU OF A HENGE MONUMENT. THIS CONSISTS OF A CIRCULAR DITCH WITH OUTER BANK INTERRUPTED BY TWO ENTRANCES, AND WAS PROBABLY USED FOR RELIGIOUS PURPOSES IN THE BRONZE AGE (ABOUT 1800 B.C.).

THIS MONUMENT IS IN THE CARE OF THE MINISTRY OF PUBLIC BUILDING AND WORKS IT IS AN OFFENCE TO INJURE OR DEFACE IT

Knowlton church has the reputation, not surprisingly, for being haunted – though since clearance of the blackthorn and scrub which enveloped it until some years ago, it is perhaps a little less magical than it once was. Yet the little ruin is still a place of mystery and romance.

CHALBURY *All Saints*

Situated near Horton on a 335ft. hill, this lovely little church, parts of which date from the 13th century, possesses one of few Georgian interiors remaining in the county. It has been sensitively preserved and is low and medieval, white-walled on the outside, with a very small squat bell-turret on a red tiled roof.

Inside is a wooden pillared entrance to the chancel with a design picked out in two shades. There is an 18th century western gallery, panelled high-sided family box pews with doors, and a three-decker pulpit. In 1976 new Communion rails were installed in memory of Sir Owen Morshead, founder of the Dorset Historic Churches Trust, a slate in the chancel recording the event. A notice states that a rector's youngest son went to Africa as a Government botanist.

Notably, a large elm tree in the churchyard was used as a navigational aid in times past (for it could be seen from the Channel), until destroyed during a storm in 1703.

Apart from the church little remains of the old village of Chalbury. The Dorset historian, Hutchins, is said to have stated that 'from here the air is clean and wholesome'.

An 18th century rector, Thomas Barford, was incumbent here for more than fifty years.

Chalbury, All Saints

7. The Chancel

Looking towards the east end of the church, one faces the chancel (or sanctuary). It contains the *Communion or Lord's Table*, the organ and choir stalls. Notice the *chancel* arch - is it Anglo-Saxon or Norman? If it is round and very ornamental it is probably Norman. If it is round but of one order only, it is Anglo-Saxon.

Priest's Door Occasionally there may be a small blocked-up door leading into the chancel from the churchyard. This was known as the *priest's door* for the chancel belonged to the priest and he had his own entrance. The remainder of the church was the responsibility of the people of the parish.

Communion Table Before the Reformation, altars were often of stone, but after the Reformation they were replaced by tables in accordance with a Royal Order issued in November 1550 during Edward VI's reign. The table was moved to the front of the chancel (as it often is today) and the

Jacobean Communion table at Radipole, St Ann

congregation stood around it during the service of Holy Communion. Elizabethan and Jacobean tables were often of lovely old oak, elaborately carved and with bulbous legs. Jacobean tables were less decorative.

Communion Rails In front of the Communion table are the *Communion rails*. These came into use in the late 16th century with the disappearance of rood screens (see below) after the Reformation. By the end of the 17th century, by order of Archbishop Laud, nearly all churches had Communion rails so that people could kneel in front of them during the Communion service in an orderly manner. They usually extend from wall to wall, but sometimes enclose the Communion table on three sides.

Houselling (Houselynge/Housling) Benches Rarely seen, these were used during the service of Holy Communion. The word comes from *'housel'* – a medieval name for 'Eucharist'. There is an example to be seen in Wimborne Minster (see chap. 4).

Chair Is there an ancient-looking chair standing on the left-hand side of the Communion table? If so, it is probably Jacobean. There may be one on the right-hand side too. The chair on the north (left) side is for the use of the Bishop when he visits the church for a Confirmation or other event. These chairs are good examples of the work of the old craftsmen.

Armchair of Bishop family, see Chilcombe, chap. 17

Reredos At the back of the Communion table is the *reredos* which is a screen or panelling, sometimes in the form of a tapestry or painting, or a piece of sculpture or metalwork. The word comes from the French "areredos" (from *arere*, behind and *dos*, back). Not many examples remain today, wooden panels or embroidered hangings having taken their place. You will easily recognize the Victorian reredos for it is often of white marble and massive. Sometimes the east window is partially blocked by the reredos, somewhat spoiling its effect.

Triptych The reredos may be in the form of a *triptych* which consists of a set of three panels or pictures, usually hinged, so that the two outer panels fold over the larger central one.

Sometimes visible above the Communion table are the letters 'A' and 'O'. These represent the first and last letters of the Greek alphabet and stand for *Alpha* (beginning) and '*Omega*' (end). They signify that Christ is the beginning and the end.

Sometimes the letters 'INRI' are to be seen. These are the initial letters of *Iesus Nazarenus Rex Iudacorum*' - Jesus of Nazareth, King of the Jews.

Frequently come across today – as a car-sticker or worn as a badge – is the *Sign of the Fish*. The initial letters of the Greek for 'Jesus Christ, Son of God, Saviour', form the Greek word for fish, and this was used as a secret sign by the early Christians.

The Ten Commandments, the Lord's Prayer, and the Creed

These may be prominently sited on either side of the Communion table, or perhaps at the back of the church. They were set up in churches during the reign of Queen Elizabeth I, by her command.

Choir Stalls 15th century choir stalls are often beautifully carved, sometimes with quaint figures of animals and birds.

Reading Desk The *reading (or prayer)* desk stands at the head of the choir stalls. From this desk the service is conducted and the prayers read.

Rood (or Chancel) Screen Is there a wooden partition in front of the chancel, stretching from side to side of the church, or between the chancel arch? This is the *rood (or chancel)* screen, its purpose being to divide the chancel from the nave. It was kept locked in medieval times for – as we have seen – only the priest and his attendants were allowed to enter the sanctuary, while the nave, which was often used for secular purposes, belonged to the people. Rood screens made of stone are fairly rare, later screens (of the 14th and 15th century) being made of oak. Of the latter, there are many lovely specimens to be seen, particularly in Devon.

Rood and Rood Loft Above the rood screen was the *rood* (the image of Christ on the cross) and sometimes there was a *loft* over the screen known as the *rood loft*. This was mainly used as accommodation for the choir and instrumentalists (or organ), and it may also have been used for preaching. Access to the rood loft was by way of a *staircase* and a *door* in the wall at the side. One sometimes comes across such a staircase, for in many churches they remain within the wall, some with their original doors. Only about twelve old rood lofts exist today in the whole of England.

Organ These instruments were used from the 10th century onwards, the earlier ones being smaller and less complicated than those in use today. By the 15th century, even some of the smaller churches possessed an organ. They were sometimes situated in the rood loft. (see above).

Before organs were electrified as most are today, they had to be hand-blown. This was usually done by a choirboy or the verger and was quite hard work. It involved occupying a small cupboard in the vestry behind the organ, pumping a wooden handle, and making sure that the metal weight on the end of a length of rope did not drop below a certain point. If the organ-blower went to sleep, the organ would run out of steam and the music would grind to a halt. Looked upon as rather a chore by most choirboys, an indication of how they filled in odd minutes between 'blowing' are the numerous initials sometimes to be seen carved into the woodwork around the blower!

Apse Occasionally the chancel may have a domed or vaulted semi-circular top end to it. This is called an apse which from Anglo-Saxon times formed the top end of the chancel. There are still examples of apsidal chancels to be seen though not a great many. (see chap. 17 Moreton)

8. The Shaftesbury Area

HAZELBURY BRYAN *St. Mary and St. James*

St Mary and St James

Dating mainly from the 15th century and sensitively restored by Sir Charles Nicholson in 1935, this spacious, well cared-for church dominates the village from a hill overlooking the Blackmore Vale. Hazelbury Bryan is said to have twice suffered from an outbreak of plague, the church of that time falling into decay, the village being burnt down and subsequently totally re-built. A small Norman church is thought to have formerly occupied the site.

The tower is well-proportioned with buttresses and a square vice (stair turret) at the north-east corner. Access to the churchyard is by way of a fine, gabled lych-gate by Mr. R. G. Parsons of Dewlish, which won an award from the Civic Trust in 1969. It was presented by Miss Violet Cross of the Manor House, a benefactress of the church. Mr. Parsons also made the heavy, panelled oak chest to be seen at the rear of the church.

The nave and north aisle have original wagon roofs, the low-pitched south aisle has moulded timbers and there is a bell-ringer platform over the vestry where the ringers are in view of the congregation. The studded west door bears date 1823.

Of particular interest is the lectern, carved by Henry Spicer, from black oak which had originally been piles in Emperor Hadrian's bridge at Newcastle-on-Tyne. It is said that the wood was probably growing as a tree when Christ was on earth. The panelled pulpit with tester (canopy) was made by local craftsmen and is 18th century; the font is 12th century with an 18th century cover. There are painted texts on the walls and fragments of medieval glass in the north-east window. The Royal Arms of Queen Anne have been altered to George I.

The village, which today has a population of just under one thousand, derives its name from Sir Guy de Bryan who purchased the Manor House in 1361. Some 400 year-old houses existing here were restored in 1939, and given by Miss Cross as homes for widows and daughters of the clergy.

WOOLLAND

This is a remote village lying beneath Bulbarrow Hill on the edge of the Blackmore Vale. The nearest links with civilization is Child Okeford three miles to the north-east and Hazelbury Bryan in the other direction. The earliest mention of it was made in 939 AD, and subsequently it was referred to in the Domesday Book as 'Wonlode' (or 'Winlande') meaning 'meadowland'.

Woolland

The little church, designed by Gilbert Scott, was erected in 1856, and replaces an old private chapel pulled down the previous year. It is said to be one of Scott's favourites. A font bowl from the 15th century comes from the old church, as does an ancient brass to Mary Argenton (1616), with an eight-line inscription.

The chancel is apsidal and vaulted, and there is a variety of stonework. The pulpit consists of a single block of Caen stone, while on the chancel columns are carvings of leaves depicting every tree to be found in Woolland and surrounding districts. To the right of the east window, a stone replica of a robin's nest represents one - which was left undisturbed by the workmen constructing the chancel until such time as the eggs had hatched out and the birds flown.

In November 1986 the spire of the church was found to be in a dangerous condition and was taken down at a cost of £5,000. An enormous yew tree 60ft high x 53ft. in diameter dominates the churchyard, apparently split at some time, though believed to have grown into its present shape of several

mighty trunks. Partly held together by an iron brace, its measurement in 1871 was 23ft. around the circumference, and more recently 31ft. It is said to be 1000 years old, with a more cautious estimate of '17th century and probably before'. Now, however, there is evidence that it could be 2,000 years old.

To the west of the church is the manor house (known to some as 'The Rectory'). Built in the reign of Elizabeth I or James I, it is large and irregular and was originally L-shaped. It was believed to have been at one time joined up with the adjacent chapel.

Woolland

IBBERTON *St. Eustace*

Mainly of the late 15th century this simple medieval church, lying below Bulbarrow Hill, is approached by way of a halter path and a climb of fifty steps. From its lofty perch on a high plateau above the Blackmore Vale, fine views are to be had of the surrounding countryside.

Ibberton

The church is thought to have been built between 1380 and 1400, the north aisle having been added c1500. The building fell into a state of decay in the mid-19th century and collapsed in 1889, when a temporary church of corrugated iron and timber was constructed in the village. Here services were held (including baptisms), though weddings had to be solemnized in the nave of the dilapidated church.

Interior

In 1902 careful restoration began, and it was re-opened by the Bishop of Salisbury in July 1909.

The pulpit was built from some 18th century panelling, and the font is 15th century with a quern at its foot, used as a font in the temporary church. In a glass case in the vestry, and of particular interest, is a chained 'black letter' copy of the Book of Homilies published in 1673, one of only eight known copies. Also to be seen are the remains of medieval and Tudor glass, a Tudor Rose, and a 17th century screen in the tower arch. A royal coat of arms of George III is of unusual shape, being painted on a wooden panel fixed on the west wall of the aisle. In the tower is a clock which is a First World War Memorial.

A large 19th century earthenware pitcher in the north aisle is believed to be Verwood pottery. At Christmas time the bell-ringers would take it around to the local farms to be filled with cider.

This church's dedication is very uncommon in this country, there being apparently only two others so dedicated. St. Eustace was a Roman general who, as a consequence of seeing a shining cross between the antlers of the stag he was hunting, became a Christian and suffered an awful death.

The village, referred to in the Domesday Book as Abristentona, was also known as Ebrictinton and Edbrichton, before becoming Ibberton.

MARNHULL *St. Gregory*

The village of Marnhull lies scattered amongst the hills overlooking Blackmore Vale. Its church, which is Norman in origin and largely rebuilt in the 15th century, has one surviving pier from this period situated in the north arcade, its capital carved with grotesque faces. It is thought that the rebuilding was

St Gregory

probably carried out by Glastonbury Abbey which owned the living until the Dissolution, and this may account for the church's splendid tower. With its 15th century canopied niches and imposing buttresses, an 18th century parapet and pinnacles, this tower is a landmark for miles around. Of the six bells which the church possesses the fifth, which has been rung for 600 years, is very valuable.

Some restoration was carried out c1880. The almost flat roof of the nave consists of carved panels, each one different, and is said to be one of the best in Dorset. A new wooden ceiling at the east end of the nave replaces an Elizabethan lath and plaster one, and obscures the top of the wall-painting over the chancel arch. This Queen Anne fresco has the Lord's Prayer inscribed on it and is noteworthy for the large black lettering showing through in one corner - the Commandments from Elizabethan times.

Three monuments, a rafter roof in the north aisle said to be of Irish Oak, a pulpit of Marnhull stone, a number of 17th century hatchments, and the Royal Stuart coat of arms over the west door are other features of this interesting church. One of the monuments (c1478) is an alabaster effigy of a knight in armour lying at rest between his two wives who are dressed in identical clothing of the time of Agincourt. Of particular note is a stone bench inside the tower porch - a relic of the days before the 13th/14th centuries when churches contained no pews. (see chap. 9). A very old and rare oak portable offertory collection box may be seen in the Hussey chapel.

Three generations of the Glisson family were rectors here for 106 years during the 17th/18th centuries. Nearby stands Nash House – a fine Tudor manor given to Katherine Parr by Henry VIII.

KINGTON MAGNA *All Saints*

Situated near to Gillingham, with extensive views over the Blackmore Vale, this village has a church with a fine, solid-looking 15th century tower with medieval bells and diagonal buttresses.

The church is mentioned by Pevsner in his 'Buildings of England', chiefly due to its 'three light window with flower tracery, baffling in some detail'.

The remainder of the church has been much restored though, as well as the tower, there are traces of earlier work including a Norman chancel.

In the vestry is a 17th century chest, and there is a large old yew tree in the churchyard.

An incumbent here for fifty-seven years (from 1768 to 1825) was John Toogood.

Kington Magna.
Dorset (diagonal buttresses)

HINTON ST. MARY *St. Peter*

Elevated and with fine views of Blackmore Vale, this church was rebuilt in 1846 except for the 15th century tower with its grotesque carvings. It possesses a good 17th century monument (of date 1655) to Thomas Freke and his wife, Thomas being the son of Robert Freke and auditor and teller of the Exchequer during the reigns of Henry VIII and

St Peter

Elizabeth I. He built the fine manor house standing adjacent to the church which passed by marriage to the Pitt family, and thus to General Pitt-Rivers, notable for his excavations of Romano-British sites.

One of the church's oldest possessions is a 700 year-old font which in olden times was locked against witches and others who were believed to steal the holy water. The register dates from 1581.

This village of thatch and local stone, situated on a hill overlooking the river Stour, was first recorded as 'Cumb-Tun' (village in a narrow valley) and 'Hamtun' in the 10th century, being mentioned in the Domesday Book as 'Haintone', and becoming Cumton Abbatisse in the 1200s and Hinton Marye in the early 1600s. With the purchase of the manor house by the abbey of St. Mary in Shaftesbury, 'St. Mary' became added to the name.

Following the Reformation, the manor house was rebuilt by Thomas Freke.

9. The Nave

The nave is, as we have seen, the main body of the church. There are usually three aisles in the nave – one in the centre and one on either side, though there may be only a central aisle or a central aisle and one at the side. The word 'aisle' comes from a 14th century word 'ele' (which comes from an old French word '*ala*') meaning 'wing' or 'side'. So, strictly speaking, there is no

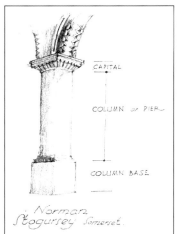

such thing as a 'central aisle' as only the side aisles can be called 'aisles'. Most of us refer to the passage up the middle of the church as the 'central aisle' though, and will probably continue to do so!

Transept Now look to the right and left of the nave and towards the chancel you will probably see what are known as *transepts*. Transepts are set at right angles to the nave and give the church its cruciform (or cross) shape.

Arcade Looking down the church towards the west end, you may see an *arcade* (or row) of arches with supporting *columns* (pillars). The pillars consist of base, shaft (or column) and *capital*. From the capital springs the arch. Arcades usually separate the nave from the aisles.

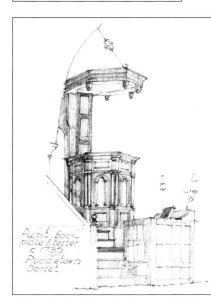

Pulpit Now take a look at the church furniture, of which the most prominent feature is probably the *pulpit*. Sermons were originally preached from the west end of the chancel and possibly from *rood lofts* (see chap. 7). In 1603, however, when preaching became a more important part of the service, it was decreed that all churches should have pulpits. Quite a number were made in the 16th/17th centuries.

Early pulpits were of oak and quite small. Pre-Reformation pulpits were often tall and narrow on a slender pedestal. Victorian pulpits were often heavy by comparison. About one hundred pre-Reformation pulpits of wood exist today. Medieval stone pulpits are mostly found in Somerset. Jacobean pulpits date from the beginning of the 17th century and were wooden and often richly carved. Many have *sounding-boards ('testers')* above, supported either by a high back or a pillar. The purpose of the tester was to help carry the preacher's voice to the back of the church.

There is an example of a sounding board and high back in St. Nicholas church, Abbotsbury (see chap.13) where the pulpit is early Jacobean or late Tudor.

Pulpit with tester (sounding board) - Cerne Abbas

Occasionally one comes across a very tall pulpit - so tall that the preacher must have felt himself to be completely isolated from the congregation. In the days when people flocked to church in large numbers, however, he would have been at eye-level with those occupying the gallery, which may extend around three sides of the church. (see chap. 13 Weymouth)

Occasionally one finds twin pulpits as in the redundant church of St. George, Portland, where the two pulpits stand halfway down at the crossing. (see chap. 14)

Three-decker Pulpit Three-decker pulpits, of which not many remain today, date from the 17th/18th centuries. They came into being along with high box-pews. (see below). During the service the parish clerk made the responses from the lowest deck, the Scriptures were read from the second, and the preacher delivered his sermon from the top deck.

Another example is the small ancient church at Winterborne Tomson, a building that has retained its complete 18th century fittings, including a two-decker pulpit and box pews. (see chap.4)

Lectern The lectern, from which the lessons are read, is situated in front of the chancel on the opposite side from the pulpit. (Before the Reformation it stood inside the chancel). The Bible rests on the ledge, and there is often an eagle with outstretched wings to represent the carrying of the Gospel to the four ends of the earth. Occasionally there is a pelican, a turkey or a gamecock instead of an eagle, and sometimes there are three lions at the base of the lectern, as though guarding the book above. About 40 brass medieval eagle lecterns remain in this country, as well as about twenty wooden ones.

Lecterns in the form of a desk on a supporting pillar may be two or four-sided and of wood or metal. Sometimes there are desks at two levels for kneeling or standing.

Pews The ends of the pews ('bench ends') may be elaborately carved, though the best examples of carved bench ends are to be seen in Somerset, Devon and Cornwall, these being flat-headed as opposed to the poppy-headed bench-ends of East Anglia.

During the 13th and 14th centuries churches contained no pews at all, the congregation having to stand throughout the service, often on a floor of bare earth covered with straw and litter. So stone benches fixed against the walls were provided for the elderly and infirm, hence the expression 'Let the weakest go to the wall'. Sometimes these benches encircle a pillar or pillars.

In the 14th century fixed seats or benches came into use consisting of thick oak planks with plain ends which later became more decorative. By the end of the 15th century, when sermons became of more importance, benches were placed in all churches.

Box-pews As we have seen, box-pews went with three-decker pulpits and were known as horse-boxes. They were often unsightly in appearance, replacing the benches with their beautifully carved bench-ends. Popular in the 18th century, they were a way of keeping out draughts, though once inside one's high box, one would not be able to see much of what was going on during the service. If the sermon was particularly long and uninteresting the occupant of a box pew could 'nod off' without being detected. Some churches with more modern pews still retain a few of their old box pews.

In medieval times patrons of churches would be given a special seat in the chancel which came to be known as the Squire's Pew. The Squire's family seat often consisted of raised pews and a staircase, and contained a table and upholstered armchair, with curtains and cushions and even a carpet fitted. A stove kept the family warm in winter, for churches were draughty and inadequately heated in those days - and some still are.

Roof These are always of wood. If they are of stone, they are called *vaults*. There are various types of roof, the most common being the *barrel* or *wagon roof* which may be seen in most churches in the south-west, sometimes having carved *bosses* which were a feature of the West Country. Sometimes they are coloured, and often carved with a variety of interesting subjects.

Other ornamental types of roof are the *king-post* and the *tie-beam*, which are sometimes decorated with bosses where the rafters intersect. The tie-beam roof has a horizontal beam which holds together two corresponding rafters.

The most ornamental type of roof is the *hammer-beam* and *double hammer-beam*, often decorated with numerous angels, sometimes numbering more than a hundred, which give the impression of being in flight. The hammer-beam roof is found only in the eastern counties, but a particularly striking roof in mock hammer-beam form and with huge bosses may be seen at Bere Regis church (see chap. 16).

Some roofs are a combination of several different types.

Crypt Crypts, (or *Undercrofts*), are sometimes to be found in cathedrals and larger churches, as for instance beneath the choir of St. Cuthberga, Wimborne Minster (see chap. 4).

10. The Sherborne Area

SANDFORD ORCAS *St. Nicholas*

This little church of Ham Hill stone, situated four miles north of Sherborne, stands close to an attractive 16th century manor house which has belonged to the Medlycott family for 250 years. It has a 15th century tower and chancel, with traces of 14th century work to be seen in the chancel and in the nave. There is an early 16th century screen, and a Norman font resembling an upturned Canterbury Bell has an oak scroll cover of the 1600s. Victorian restoration took place in 1871.

In the small south chapel exist several monuments to the Hutchings family, but of particular interest is a wall monument of alabaster, carved and

13th cent. font with 17th cent. oak cover. Sandford Orcas Dorset.

painted, to William Knoyle dated 1607. He wears armour and kneels between his two wives and their eleven children, those of the first lying stiff and dead on a skull behind their mother, the other seven kneeling in black gowns. An inscription states that he married 'fillip, daughter of Robert Morgane by whom hee had yssve 4 children and bee dead.'

The first part of the village's name derives from Saxon times when water from three streams was forded over a sandy base. In Norman times the manor came into the ownership of a family known as Orescuilz, from which the second part of the name derives. Until 1896 Sandford Orcas was in Somerset.

TRENT *St. Andrew*

At the entrance to the churchyard of this 14th century church the large building, now a private dwelling, was originally the home of the chantry priest. No sign of the chantry chapel now remains. The stone spire atop the church tower is unusual for Dorset.

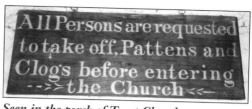

Seen in the porch of Trent Church

In the porch a quaint old notice requests that 'All persons... take off pattens and clogs before entering'. Inside, an ornate carved pulpit dating from 1600 was brought over from Holland by a former rector. There is a late medieval rood screen and some early 16th century bench ends. An unusual feature is the wording over the archway of the Manor chapel in the north transept. In looking-glass writing, it reads: 'All flesh is grass and the glory of it as the floure of the feilde' - its purpose apparently being to remind the young ladies of the manor of their vanity when they looked in their mirrors instead of listening to the sermon.

Also of interest are the pre-Reformation (early 1500s) pews carved with symbols in such a way that four put together form the prayer, 'AVE MARIA GRATIA PLENA DOMINUS TECUM AMEN'. It is said that when Cromwell's soldiers were approaching Trent, the villagers thought the church would be burnt down if the Latin prayer was discovered. So they unscrewed the pews and mixed them up, and thus they remained until quite recently when one group was returned to its original position.

Apart from its Royal visitor (Charles II fled to Trent disguised as a servant after the battle of Worcester and took refuge in a priest's hole in Trent Manor), Trent has a more recent claim to fame. In 1962 the village became the retirement home of Lord Fisher of Lambeth (1887-1972) and Lady Fisher, when they were offered the use of Trent Rectory for their lifetime. The Archbishop frequently conducted services at Trent and remained there until his death when he was interred in a magnificent Victorian vault. The stone slab commemorating the ninety-ninth Archbishop of Canterbury may be seen in the churchyard, close to a cross with a circular base and modern steps.

Beside the church, invisible from the road, stands the Manor House, and there are four almshouses built by Mary Turner, wife of the former rector.

STOURTON CAUNDLE *St. Peter*

Stourton Caundle

This brown stone village with a clear stream flowing through, the Caundle brook, and thatched cottages, is one of four Caundle villages situated in the Blackmore Vale, the others being Bishop's Caundle, Purse Caundle and Caundle Marsh. Its small church with a 15th century tower, some ancient bells, and outward-leaning walls, stands on slightly elevated ground almost in a farmyard. With a history going back 700 years, it was restored in 1899, but remains unspoiled.

The interior is whitewashed and contains a 13th century chancel and a 15th century nave with a plastered wagon roof. There is a little wooden 17th century pulpit with 15th century traceried panels, an 18th century font with cover, and a Jacobean communion rail. On the south side is a small chapel accessed by way of a 13th century arch.

The village derives its name from 'caundle' meaning a hill chain, and from the Stourton family who lived in the county in the 15th century.

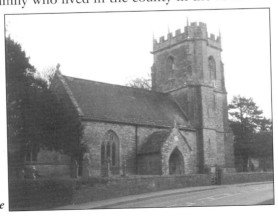

Bishop's Caundle

SHERBORNE ABBEY *St. Mary*

Famous for its public school and its castle, the attractive town of Sherborne is also noted for its fine Abbey Church, founded by King Ine for St. Aldhelm in 705, at which time the large diocese of Winchester was split into two. Of Saxon origin with alteration by the Normans, further re-building commenced under Abbot John Brunyng from 1415-36, and continued under Abbot William

Sherborne Abbey

Bardford (1436-59). The Abbey became a parish church following the Dissolution, and in 1849 restoration of the nave, transepts and aisles by the Digby family took place. The great tower and the transept arches are still mainly Norman.

The reredos in the Lady Chapel is by Laurence Whistler, and in the choir stalls are 15th century carvings including a monkey eating acorns and a boy being chastised. There are some good monuments and Purbeck marble effigies of abbots from the 13th century, as well as altar tombs to Sir John Horsey and his son (1546 and 1564), to the Lewestons, husband and wife (1584), and a splendid monument to John Digby, Earl of Bristol (1698) with his two wives.

West window

The Abbey is particularly noted for its intricate and beautiful fan vaulting with its seventy-five bosses, and not to be missed is the new stained-glass Great West window (by local Artist John Hayward) which was dedicated by the Queen in 1998. This window replaced a Victorian one attributed to Pugin, and there was some controversy over its installation, though the Abbey won!

HOLWELL *St. Lawrence*

Situated by the Caundle Brook just south of Bishop's Caundle, this brown-stoned 15th century Perpendicular church possesses a fine tower and a number of horrific gargoyles. Restored in 1885, it has two original panelled roofs, the one in the nave being a barrel roof with a cornice adorned with Tudor roses, the other in the north aisle, timber and carved with foliage and stars. On one of the beams is written in medieval lettering, 'Jo London'. Did John of London, reflects Arthur Mee in his *Dorset*, give this roof when he retired to Holwell? Or did the builder, pleased with his handiwork, write his name upon it? Various medieval and Victorian carved faces adorn the walls, and clear glass windows give light to the building. An inscription on panelling near the organ is to a now vanished gallery and reads, 'Ion Chaffie gave a Tree to ye Erecting of this Gallery 1734.' The pulpit dates from the end of the reign of Elizabeth I, and there is an hourglass on the wall near to it.

This church is mentioned by Nikolaus Pevsner in his Buildings of England series, with particular reference to the big gargoyles and 'embattled aisles'. The village was once recorded as being a detached part of Somerset which became incorporated with Dorset. Its name is derived from the old English for 'ridge' or 'bank in a hollow'.

Situated by the churchyard wall are the village stocks.

Stocks at Holwell

Folke

FOLKE *St. Lawrence*

Turning south from Allweston, one arrives at the tiny village of Folke with its attractive church standing adjacent to mainly 17th century Folke Manor, the latter having a fine staircase.

Well worth seeking out, the church is in Traditional style, rebuilt and re-furbished in 1628, with embattled aisles and a square tower. It appears Gothic from the outside though showing Classical influence within. Some of its oak seats have shell-back terminals on their bench ends, and there are oak screens in the chancel and the north aisle. The small basin font is of stone with a contemporary oak cover. Of particular interest is the hourglass stand in the pulpit.

Over the centuries the name of this village has varied between Folk, Folke, Foolke, and Fowlke, the name deriving from *folc*, i.e. freeholders.

LILLINGTON *St. Martin*

Surprisingly isolated considering its proximity to Sherborne, this tiny village has a church standing on rising ground, adjacent to an old barn dating from c1600. From the churchyard fine views are to be had looking across open country above Beer towards the valley of the Wriggle.

Lillington

An embattled, six-pinnacled 15th century tower surmounts the church, its corners ornamented with large griffins alternating with smaller gargoyles. There is a square turret staircase. Two steps lead down through a nail-studded north door to the interior which is narrow and limewashed and attractive in its simplicity, with no division between chancel (15th century) and nave. Features of interest include the plaster barrel roof, an early 16th century octagonal font with a 17th century cover, and many monuments to the Gallop family. There are some late medieval consecration crosses in the walls.

Another point of interest is the church's connection with Sir Walter Raleigh who had married secretly c February 1589, Elizabeth Throckmorton, one of Queen Elizabeth I's maids-of-honour. Their eldest son, Damrei, was born on 29th March 1592 but died in infancy. The following year, another son, Walter, was born and was baptised at Lillington on 1st November 1593. The register in which this event was recorded has long since been lost, though the entry: '*Walter, son of S.W. Rahley*', can still be seen in the Bishop's Transcripts, a copy of which hangs on the south wall of the church.

It is considered that the baptism took place in this out-of-the-way village rather than in Sherborne Abbey because it was still necessary for Sir Walter (a favourite of the Queen) to maintain a measure of discretion following her displeasure at the discovery of his marriage. Young Walter grew up a headstrong youth and much to the grief of his parents was killed in 1617 whilst leading an attack in Guiana.

LONGBURTON *St. James the Great*

The village of Longburton is spread out on either side of the Roman Road which runs from Dorchester to Sherborne. Its church is mainly of the 15th century, but has a 13th century squat tower which appears to have sunk into the high gabled roof – in spite of having been heightened in the 17th century with parapet and gargoyles.

St James the Great

'Curse not the King, noe, not in thy thought', runs the inscription (taken from Ecclesiastes) under the royal arms of 1662 situated over the south doorway. Equally striking is the quotation: 'Feare thou the lord and the King and medelle not with them that are given to change'. (Proverbs 24,21) – no doubt dating from the Civil War and a plea by Charles I for support.

Moving on to the north chapel, one finds two large canopied monuments, colourful and recently restored. One, comprising two recumbent figures – a man in armour with his head on a book, and his wife in ruff, gown and cloak – is to the memory of Sir Henry and Lady Winston of Standish in Gloucestershire, who lived during the reign of Elizabeth I. Their daughter, Eleanor Fitzjames of nearby Leweston, requested that monuments to her parents' memory be installed at Longburton, her husband's parish, a similar request having been turned down by Standish.

The second monument commemorates Sir John Fitzjames (in 17th century armour) and his wife, Joan, parents of Leweston Fitzjames, who married Eleanor. There is a connection here with Sir Winston Churchill, Eleanor's sister, Sarah, having married John Churchill of Glanvilles Wootton, the couple becoming grandparents of the notable John Churchill, Duke of Marlborough, ancestor of Sir Winston.

In the north aisle vestry, the Longburton turret clock is a relic of the late 17th century, entries in the churchwardens' accounts referring to payments for 'keeping ye clock'. It was repaired and restored in 1972. Thomas Bartholomew, the maker, was also responsible for the one (still in working order) at nearby Yetminster. Clocks of this type would have needed to be wound every day or on alternate days, no doubt with outsize keys.

From the churchyard there is a pleasant view across fields, looking towards a rambling, partly 15th, partly late-16th century house known as West Hall.

HOLNEST *St. Mary*

This church, with no village nearby, stands isolated in a field, though it is clearly visible from the main road. Some years ago it was saved from becoming a ruin by the efforts of parishioners and others. Mainly of the 15th century, it is constructed of five blocks of different centuries cleverly fitted together. The interior is attractive, with white-painted box pews having candle sconces.

The chancel is 19th century and there is a 13th century font. The pulpit at one time had a sounding board. There is clear glass of good quality in the windows. The churchyard has heavy Gothic cast iron gates.

Some consecration crosses still survive (see chap.20).

Holnest, St Mary

MINTERNE MAGNA *St. Andrew*

This unspoiled village of mellowed stone cottages lies between High Stoy and Dogbury Hills. Its little church, built of local materials and Ham Hill stone, stands close to the road, and is crowded with memorials, one being to the Napier family, well-known in Dorset. Sir Nathaniel's monument is large and he lies adjacent to his father, Sir Robert, who held the position of Chief Baron of the Exchequer for Ireland and built an almshouse in Dorchester which he called 'Napper's Mite'.

Minterne Magna

Other monuments, which are reminders of famous families who have lived in the village, include one to Charles Churchill, son of an earlier Winston Churchill and a brother of the Duke of Marlborough who fought at Blenheim and died aged 56 in 1714. The Digby family are also represented, Admiral Sir Henry Digby, who commanded a ship at Trafalgar, being commemorated in brass.

The church is based on an original Saxon building. The chancel and nave were built in the first half of the 15th century and the north chapel was added c1610-20. The tower was rebuilt in 1800 and Gothicized, further alterations being made to it in 1894 when it was heightened. The organ was moved from the chancel and re-sited in 1963.

Minterne Magna is part of a new benefice formed in 2002, which includes Cerne Abbas, Godmanstone and Buckland Newton. Minterne House, with its park and woodland garden of trees and flowering shrubs, stands close to the church.

HERMITAGE *St. Mary*

St Mary

This village, lying at the foot of High Stoy, a hill 860ft. high, is well-named - for its houses and farms are tucked away out of sight, and its population is only 80. The little church is called 'The Hermitage' the name said to have derived from some Augustinian friars who settled here, perhaps in the 12th century, in what was then known as the Forest of Blackmore. Under the direct protection of the king, they received grants of land from Edward II.

In later years, when there was no more forest, the church became a perpetual curacy in the gift of the Duchy of Cornwall and at the present time it is one of the five parishes which make up the High Stoy group. Restored in the 17th century, it was largely rebuilt c1800, complete with barrel roof and attractive Queen Anne bell-cote with a knob on top, which replaced the original tower. The latter contained, somewhat strangely, an apartment for the use of the curate and there was once said to have been a room over the porch which was used for storing wood for the curate's fire.

During the Second World War, a Bournemouth art gallery hung several of its large pictures within the building for safe keeping.

Interior

MELBURY BUBB *St. Mary*

Reached by way of narrow winding roads apparently leading nowhere, this village is tiny and comprises a little church backed by thickly-wooded Bubb Down, a few cottages and a farm or two. The name is said to derive from Melbury, a many-coloured hill and Bubb an old family name.

The font in the church is a curiosity. A very early example of Dorset art of the first half of the 11th century, it is believed to be part of a sculptured Anglo-Saxon cross or column, the lower end having been hollowed out to form the basin. Around its sides, intertwined with tendrils, are representations of a lion, a wolf, a horse and a stag. Why was *Melbury Bubb* not the other end of the column used, is the question sometimes asked - for the creatures are the wrong way up!

One explanation is that the sculpture was intended to signify 'that all cruelty shall cease through the influence of Christ' – or it could have been purely accidental. In his *Dorset*, Arthur Mee puts a different interpretation upon the carvings, describing them as a 'bold and handsome circle of hounds chasing deer, with wild beasts preying on each other'.

The tower, with shafts and a frieze, dates from the 15th century, but in 1851 the remainder of the church was rebuilt in 15th century style, some original windows being retained and some excellent original glass – some of the best in Dorset, it is said - preserved and incorporated. Above the modern east window may be seen smaller fragments of old glass incorporating the eagle, the lion, the bull and the angel of the four evangelists. There are carved oak bench ends and a chancel screen.

In the churchyard are some interesting old tombs, one dating from 1568 and another having an epitaph to Richard Handleigh who died in 1646 and was rector of the church for 59 years. (see chap. 3 Epitaph).

An Elizabethan manor house, considerably rebuilt in the early 17th century, stands adjacent to the church, and is now a farm. This is an exceedingly peaceful and unfrequented spot.

MELBURY SAMPFORD St. Mary

This 15th century cruciform church lies close to Melbury House in magnificent parkland with massive oaks, chestnuts and limes. It was drastically restored in the 19th century by Lord Ilchester. Lions, wolves, and gargoyles with wings and horns decorate the top of the tower, guarding the family tombs and monuments.

The chancel walls are enriched with carvings and inlaid marble, and a fine reredos depicts the Last Supper. There is some good stained glass in the windows, one being of the 16th century.

Other features include two canopied tombs under the four arches of the tower, with alabaster knights in armour, one being to Egidius Strangwaies (Strangways) and his wife Dorothy, the other to the Brownings who preceded the Strangways. A figure of a kneeling woman, by the sculptor Chantrey, is to the memory of Lady Ilchester, and on a table tomb lies a young man, Denzil Fox Strangways with his little Skye terrier sitting at his feet.

The two families, the Brownings and the Strangways, are commemorated in tablets on the walls.

There is an unusual font here with three corners, let into a pier of one of the towers.

St Mary

STOCKWOOD *St. Edwold*

Situated in its tiny parish below Bubb Down, in a wooded valley adjacent to a 17th century farmhouse, this is one of the smallest churches in England. It measures approximately 30ft. by 12ft, and is the only church in the country dedicated to St. Edwold (younger brother of Edmund, king of East Anglia in the 9th century) who settled at Cerne and was buried there a year later.

Stockwood

Though probably having a pre-Norman foundation (in view of its dedication), nave and chancel were built in the early 15th century. The interior is in a state of disrepair and there is little to be seen in the way of original furnishings, these having disappeared at the 18th century restoration. The 17th century Communion table has a modern marble top and comes from Whitcombe (also in the care of The Churches Conservation Trust), though font, communion rails and pews are late Victorian. The western porch was added in 1636, and the unusual bell-turret comprises a large stone dome with pinnacles and a ball terminal, supported on four short columns. The small bell was purchased in 1877.

Access to churchyard and church is through a field gate and via a small brick footbridge - the original access. If locked, the key to the church is available from the farmhouse.

The village's earlier name was Stoke St. Edwold, and in its time it has passed through the hands of several great Dorset families. After being a separate living for many centuries, it was united in 1888 with Melbury Sampford and Melbury Osmond, though after many years of disuse it is now in the care of The Churches Conservation Trust (formerly the Redundant Churches Fund). It forms part of the Ilchester estates.

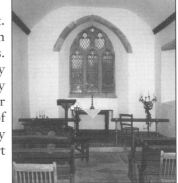

Interior

YETMINSTER *St. Andrew*

A church is said to have existed here for one thousand years or more, though very little has survived from early times. The Minster of St. Andrew, a large and imposing stone building, is Perpendicular and Early English in style and dates from the 1400s. On top of the tower, a gilded weathercock is of the 18th century.

St Andrew

There is much of interest inside this church. Affixed to the west wall of the south aisle is the base of a 12th century Purbeck marble font, while two alabaster cloaked figures standing in the east window of the north aisle are believed to be part of an ancient reredos. A 10th century cross on the north wall of the 13th century chancel is notable for its carved figure wearing a halo – a feature common in the north, though unique in the south-west. Amongst the monuments is a brass to Sir John Horsey, esquire to Henry VIII, buried here in 1531. In a recess Bridget Minterne, who died in 1649, is kneeling at a desk. There is a wagon roof over the nave which is spacious and airy with clear glass.

Several times a day the bells of the church chime the National Anthem. Installed to celebrate the Jubilee of Queen Victoria, they belong to a faceless, 300 year-old clock of 1682 made by Thomas Bartholomew, the Sherborne clockmaker who was responsible for the one at Longburton. (see chap. 10). Until 1986 when it became automatic, a team of village men climbed the fifty or so steps to the belfry daily, for the purpose of winding the three movements of this ancient time-piece and keeping the chimes going.

There are several consecration crosses, marking the church's consecration in 1310, on the external walls, and there is a scratch dial on a buttress. The churchyard contains a number of fine table tombs and headstones.

RYME INTRINSECA *St. Hippolytus*

This church was built in the late 17th century but has an Early English chancel. In the nave are some 13th century features from the original fabric, including some medieval windows. The plain font is probably early 17th century, its cover dated 1637, and there are two lance windows and green and purple cathedral glass.

The dedication is unusual, there being only one other church in the country, St. Ippolytes near Hitchin, Hertfordshire, so named – though there are a number of similar dedications in France. Born in 170 A.D. this little-known saint was the gaoler in charge of St. Laurence who was roasted on a gridiron. (see Upwey, St. Laurence). Apparently the example set by the saint so impressed Hypolite that he became a convert to the Christian faith. He died in Sardinia c235 and his feast day is 13th August.

This church was included in the List of Buildings of Special Architectural or Historic Interest in the 1961 Nationwide Survey. The unusual name of the village means 'a place on the inner rim or edge of a ridge'. (*Intrinseca* – inside; *Rima* – old English for border or rim). Thus we have a settlement within a sheltered place. Apparently 'Intrinseca' was not added until the 15th century when it was necessary to distinguish between 'In-Ryme' and 'Out-Ryme'. At that time, the lord of the manor of Ryme owned properties at Long Bredy, Langton Herring, Hermitage Hammoon and Sturminster Newton, these lands being known collectively as Ryme Extrinseca (outside). They were eventually sold off, leaving only Ryme Intrinseca.

St Hippolytus

11. Some Items of Special Interest

Take a look around the chancel again and see if you can locate any of the following objects.

Piscina Is there a shallow bowl or basin set into the south wall? If so, this is a *piscina*, once used by the priest for washing his hands before celebrating the Mass, and for washing the chalice and paten afterwards. The water was carried away down through the floor into the churchyard by way of a hollow pillar. (If you see a piscina in another part of the church, do not be confused. This indicates that there was once another altar there).

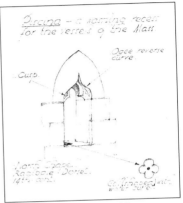

Credence Table Near to the piscina may be a small stone shelf on which was placed the bread and wine during the Mass. This was called a *credence table*.

Aumbry Also nearby may be a plain oblong opening which would originally have had a door. This is known as an *aumbry* and it was here that the vessels were stored.

Sedilia There may be a *sedilia* on the south side of the chancel. Situated to the west of the piscina, it consists of a group of two, three or four seats each called a *sedile* and often of varying heights. These would have been occupied by the priest, the deacon and the sub-deacon respectively, and - if there was a fourth - by the clerk.

Hagioscope A narrow window (usually without glass) cut at an angle through wall at the side of the chancel is known as a *hagioscope or squint*, and its purpose was to enable people sitting in the aisles and transepts to get a

view of the chancel during Mass and view the elevation of the host. There may be a hagioscope on either side of the chancel, or even a double hagioscope. The word comes from the Greek, '*I see the Holy things*'. There are many examples to be seen for they are quite common.

Now step down into the nave and look around at the walls.

Hagioscope

Clerestory These windows (pronounced 'clear-storey') are additional ones inserted above an aisle. Their purpose is to give extra lighting where a side aisle has been added at a later date, if its roof is lower than that of the nave.

Corbels These were short pieces of wood or stone projecting from walls to carry weights, such as roof trusses. They are often carved and are worth noting. Frequently depicted were the 'Man with the headache' grasping his forehead and the 'Man with the tooth-ache' clutching his jaw. Examples of these may be seen in Bere Regis church. (see chap. 16) They were probably intended as a warning against the deadly sins of gluttony and drunkenness.

Fresco Are there any *frescoes* (otherwise known as *murals* or *wall-paintings*) to be seen? These exist from medieval times and often need restoring or 'touching up' when the plaster which has covered them for centuries is removed. Subjects frequently painted were St. George and the dragon and St. Michael weighing a soul in the balance.

One sometimes comes across a wall-painting representing *St. Christopher* (the *'Christ-Bearer'*) carrying the Christ-child. According to legend, St. Christopher was a heathen giant who, on turning Christian, was instructed by a holy hermit to carry travellers over a dangerous ford. One stormy night he discovered that he had been carrying the child Jesus on his shoulder. These frescos are usually very large and cover the part of the north wall which faces the south door of the church. The reason for this is that in medieval times people were very superstitious and it was thought to be lucky to see St. Christopher on entering a church. Tarrant Crawford (chap. 4) and Winterborne Steepleton (chap. 17) have some very extensive frescoes.

Fresco-painting is a very old craft going right back to the times when cavemen painted the walls of their caverns. They needed to be painted extremely quickly, for it was necessary for the plaster on which they were placed to be damp and newly laid.

Stone carvings One comes across many examples of stone carvings in old churches, some of which give ornamentation and additional beauty to pulpits and choir stalls, while others are quaint, weird, humorous or grotesque. Many carvings depict hunting and farm scenes, animals, figures, quaint heads (perhaps of the reigning monarch, an abbot or a patron), or incidents from everyday life. Sometimes there are representations of the seven virtues and the seven deadly sins, and occasionally a mason would carve his own portrait.

Windows In early times, these were small and high up in the walls and

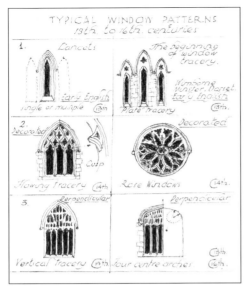

TYPICAL WINDOW PATTERNS
13th to 16th centuries

1. Lancets

The beginning of window tracery.

Early English
single or multiple (13th)

Plate tracery

Wimborne Minster, Dorset. Early English (13th)

2. Decorated

Cusp

Flowing tracery (14th)

Decorated

Rose Windows (14th)

Decorated

3. Perpendicular

Vertical tracery (15th)

Perpendicular

Four centre arches (15th)

(16th)

filled with either horn or wooden shutters to keep out draughts. In the 12th century they were narrow and set well back in the wall, the object being to keep out the weather but admit more light. Tall narrow windows known as *lancets* are Early English and date from c1220.

Later in time windows increased in size. In the 14th century the art of glass-painting was discovered and *stained-glass* windows came into being. Examples of old stained glass still remain. The decorative shapes in windows are known as tracery, and are formed by curved bars and filled with stained glass. Originally the shapes were geometrical, but developed later into flowing curves. A striking example of modern stained glass is to be seen in St. Nicholas Church, Moreton (see chap. 17). When the church was damaged by bombs in 1940, and all the stained glass destroyed, it was replaced in 1950 with fourteen stained-glass windows by *Laurence Whistler*, five of which are in the apsidal chancel. Particularly lovely and well worth seeing are the small engravings of a bombed church, fishing boat, and harvest.

Rose Window In Gothic architecture, the *Rose Window* is circular, and traceried to resemble a rose. It is sometimes called a *wheel window*.

Alms Box These boxes were provided by order of Queen Elizabeth I in 1559 and were called the *Poor Man's Box* or *Chest*. Quite a number of old alms boxes remain today, earlier ones being made from hollowed pieces of tree trunk banded with iron. Later ones were carved or made of metal, or even stone. Some are noted for their intricate construction which renders their contents completely safe. 17th century alms boxes which are quite numerous sometimes bear the words 'Remember the Poor'.

Armour From Edward II's reign every parish was called upon to provide and equip soldiers for home service. Their armour was kept in the church in charge of the churchwardens, ready for use when needed. Following the death of an important person such as the lord of the manor, his helmet, gauntlets, spurs, banners, pennons, and coat of arms were hung above his tomb in the church. As the originals were expensive copies of them were made and though many have disappeared you will still find them in some churches.

Brass Tablets These may exist from the 12th century up to the 17th, the earlier ones often being life-size. The very earliest brass is dated 1277. Only the wealthy could afford brass tablets

Brasses

at burial, though later, when cheaper substitutes were used, they became more widespread. They consist of thin metal pieces let into the stone floor of the church, the engraving being filled with a black substance. Often mats are placed over them for protection. There are about 10,000 brasses remaining in this country today and they can teach us a lot about the history of armour and costume. For instance, a sword slung in front of a knight indicates the period of the Wars of the Roses.

Brasses at Puddletown

Brass-rubbing is an inexpensive and rewarding hobby, and the results are often clearer than the original.

In the 12th and 13th centuries, stone coffins were in use for the wealthy, who were sometimes buried inside the church, the coffin-lid forming part of the floor.

Chest Ancient *chests* were important items of furniture in medieval times and there are still examples from the 12th century onwards. They are often strongly bound in iron and some have three locks or even more, all with different keys. Each key would have been in the possession of two or more church officials so that no one on their own could open the chest. In them were kept the churchwardens' accounts, wills and, after the Reformation, the parish registers, though most of these have now been transferred to the County Record Offices. Sometimes chests had rings for lifting by means of a chain or rope attached to a pole.

Church Registers Permanent records were first ordered to be kept in 1538 (though actual entry in a book was not enjoined until 1598), and some churches still have their registers intact. A short break in the church registers in the mid-1600s could have been a result of the outbreak of plague, when all those who could read and write may have been wiped out.

Churchwardens' Staves These are affixed to the two pews on either side of the central aisle, usually about half-way down the nave. Churchwardens are guardians of the parish and their staves may be surmounted by a crown or a mitre, or bear emblems connected with the church.

Church Plate This includes the chalice and paten. The chalice is the cup used for the wine and the paten the plate for the bread during the service of Holy Communion. Being valuable, the church plate is usually kept locked up so that visitors may not be able to see it.

Incumbents, List of In old churches, these lists of former rectors or vicars often go back to the 1200s. The prefix 'Sire' does not imply a title, but is merely a form of 'Sir'.

Offertory Box The offertory (collection) was not always taken during church services as it is today. Expenses were usually covered by what was known as the *church rate*. When collections were taken, however, wooden shovels or copper ladles with wooden handles were sometimes used instead of the collecting plate. Some still remain from the 17th century.

Effigy Huge box-like tombs with sculptured figures lying on top are called effigies and they are usually life-size. They do not necessarily portray the deceased person before death; sometimes they represent him (or her) when much younger. When the effigy is a knight in armour, his feet may rest on a lion (representing bravery), or in the case of a woman, on a dog (representing faithfulness). If the legs of the knight are crossed, this is sometimes said to indicate that he fought in the Crusades, though as cross-legged effigies exist from later dates this would seem not necessarily to be the case.

In Mappowder church (see chap.16) exists a very small effigy of a knight in

Effigy

chain mail with crossed legs and holding his heart in his hand to indicate that it was buried apart from his body. There are only seven little cross-legged effigies in this country. Coming more up to date, in Wareham St Martin(see chap.2) is the well-known effigy of T.E. Lawrence (the famous Lawrence of Arabia) by Eric Kennington. The most usual material used was alabaster, stone (including Purbeck marble) and occasionally wood.

Hatchment This is a painting on a lozenge-shaped board, usually 4/5ft. square, which was hung in front of a dwellinghouse for several months following a death, after which it was placed in the church. The painting consists of a shelf on which the armorial bearings, crest and motto of the deceased appear. The word 'Resurgas', meaning '*I will rise again*', often occurs, and the background is either black, or half black and half white, according to whether the deceased was married, a widower, widow, bachelor or spinster. If the left side is black and the right side white, the deceased died before his wife. If the reverse is the case, the wife died first. Hatchments were introduced in the second half of the 17th century and occur quite frequently.

Hatchment

Hatchment in Stourton Caundle Church

Monuments These often remain even though a church may have been rebuilt. They are interesting in that they provide local interest and give an insight into varying fashions throughout the ages – as, for instance, armour in the case of a knight, and dress and head-dress in the case of a lady. (The most magnificent monuments are of bronze, as for example, the royal monuments in Westminster Abbey and Canterbury Cathedral, the latter to the Black Prince). Kneeling children at the foot of a monument represent submission to parents.

Holy water stoup Inside the main entrance to the church, or perhaps inside the porch, there may be a basin in a stone niche. This is a *holy water stoup* (or *stoop*) which in medieval times would have contained water. On entering the church, people would dip their fingers into it and make the sign of the Cross as a reminder of their baptismal vows.

Holy water stoup in porch

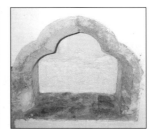

Holy water stoup

Royal Arms The royal arms are often seen displayed, perhaps opposite the main door. They were a symbol of loyalty to the crown and were usually painted on panels or carved in wood, stone or plaster. Royal arms were introduced into churches after Henry VIII became head of the Church of England, though nearly all were destroyed in the reign of Queen Mary. After that they increased in number again until the time of the Commonwealth when many were destroyed once more. From 1660 it became compulsory to display royal arms, though the practice decreased in the 19th century and gradually died out.

Particularly common are the arms of Charles II. These were sometimes updated by the simple expedient of changing the 'C' into a 'G' for George I, and a '1' added for George II.

Sedilia. 13th cent.
Rumden · Northants

12. Around Bridport and Beaminster

BEAMINSTER *St. Mary*

This town church, mainly rebuilt c1500, is in Perpendicular style with a fine and dominant west tower built in yellow Ham Hill stone, pinnacled and canopied, and topped by a weather-cock. Of Somerset style, it is said to be one of the finest in the county, even in the country. On its west front, niches and sculptures represent the Madonna, the Crucifixion, the Resurrection, and the Ascension. Less gloriously, men were hanged from it in 1685.

Beaminster

Restored in 1860, the interior is less striking, though the arcade of the 13th century has attractively carved capitals. There are two large monuments to the Strodes of Parnham and brasses of the 16th to 18th centuries. The richly carved pulpit is Jacobean; the square bowl of the font on a modern base dates from the 12th century and came from the original Norman church. The east window is of 1851 and there is some Victorian glass. An old gargoyle in the form of a crocodile's head (a subject rarely chosen by medieval craftsmen) looks down from the wall in the south aisle.

At a lower level than the churchyard are almshouses of 1630 built by Sir John Strode of Parnham House for the boarding and lodging of six poor people.

NETHERBURY *St. Mary*

This 14th/15th century well-restored Perpendicular church stands on rising ground at the north end of the village which lies off the beaten track and is approached by way of a narrow lane from the Bridport/ Beaminster road. A good view of the church - situated high on the hillside - is obtainable from the point where the river Brit passes under a bridge in the valley.

Netherbury

The building's most striking monument is believed to be to a member of the More family who died c1420 - though the alabaster figure of a knight in armour with a helmet on top of his canopied tomb is somewhat battered. The More family came from Melplash Court, a Tudor manor situated about two miles south-east of the village.

Also to be seen are brasses to the Hood family, a reminder of Admiral Sir Samuel Hood who fought under Nelson at Santa Cruz and the Nile, and of his two brothers, who were christened in Netherbury church at its ancient font. Other points of interest in the church are the beautiful Elizabethan pulpit of inlaid oak and the large square font (mentioned above) of the late 12th century. There is a drawing of this font in Dorchester Museum, which shows it without its base and standing on higher pillars. A clock in the church tower may date from as early as 1700 and is apparently still in good working order.

In the reign of King Edgar, Netherbury was designated *Netherburie* and at the time of the Domesday Book was known as *Niderberie*. It was once one of the largest parishes in Dorset for until 1847 it included Melplash, and up to 1849 Beaminster with Mapperton attached. It is worth noting the fluctuating population of the village – 1,152 in 1811, 2,162 in 1841, decreasing to 782 in 1951.

POWERSTOCK

This village (Poorstock, as it was once known) lies south-west of Toller Porcorum and Toller Fratrum. Situated amid hills and valleys, it stands high on a hill, and from its walled churchyard one looks down on a number of cottages, thatched or otherwise, scattered over hill and dale.

Powerstock

The church is mid-12th century, its most striking feature being its superb though not very symmetrical semi-circular Norman chancel arch, built of local stone and heavily ornamented. There is a 15th century south doorway, on one side of which is a king (Good King Wenceslas) with a book in his hand, and on the other a queen (Elizabeth of Hungary) with bread. A double squint (or hagioscope) on the south side of the chancel is also of interest, as is a 13th century font which was at one time relegated to the churchyard.

Powerstock chancel arch

There was considerable restoration in the Victorian era, at which time the galleries were removed and the chancel rebuilt. The lower part of the tower is Norman, but the doorway and upper part are 14th century. All the stained glass dates from the last half of the 19th century.

A rare feature of the churchyard is the 13th century dole table standing on the left-hand side of the path leading from the main entrance. From this ancient table charitable doles of bread would have been distributed to the poor and needy.

Also of interest in the north-west corner of the churchyard is the grave of Kenneth Allsop, writer and broadcaster. He lived in the adjacent hamlet of West Milton and from 1970 until his death in 1973 owned Milton Mill, now the home of the High Sheriff of Dorset.

Carving at Powerstock

LODERS *St. Mary Magdalene*

Loders

This is an attractive village with a church standing in a walled churchyard and well-kept garden. Overlooking the church and situated on the site of an old priory is 18th century Loders Court, from 1921 to 1961 the home of the late Colonel Sir Edward and Lady Le Breton. A bell cast in 1641 is a memorial to the couple who were regular worshippers. It weighs a ton and hung in the tower for nearly 300 years. In 1927, to save it from being melted down, it was placed where it now stands.

There is much of interest in the church which contains features from four centuries. Saxon work on the north wall of the nave and chancel is evidence of the existence of an earlier ecclesiastical building on the site. Recorded history begins early in the 12th century, at which time the manor belonged to one Richard de Redvers, Earl of Devon, who had connections with the abbey of St. Mercy de Montburg in Normandy. When the abbey ran into financial difficulties, he presented it with the manor of Loders. The small contingent of French monks from Montburg, who took possession of the village at this time, brought with them, it is believed, the art of cider-making. They grew their apples in what was known as Priory Orchard lying to the south-west of the church, over what was once the railway line.

A number of discoveries have been made in the church, including a large recess at the east end of the chancel wall which, when excavated, proved to be an Easter Sepulchre. Another find was a skeleton so decayed that only the lower leg bones were intact. The remains were placed in a lead casket, along with a copy of the Bridport News and a box of contemporary coins, and re-buried. Also dug up from beneath the pavement of the chapel was a 13th century Calvary Group.

Finally, the church registers date from 1636 and contain records of 4,004 burials in the churchyard. With the previous burials of which there are no records, it is estimated that the churchyard holds the remains of some 10,000 bodies. The registers also disclose that in 1883 the population of Loders was 1,105, which figure has today been reduced to a mere 500.

WHITCHURCH CANONICORUM *St.Wite (or St. Candida) and Holy Cross.*

The village of Whitchurch Canonicorum is dominated by the perpendicular buttressed tower (built c1400) of its church which claims to have been founded by Alfred the Great. Whether its name derives from the fact that it was built of stone rather than wood or because of its connections with St.Wite, is not known.

For many centuries Whitchurch Canonicorum was a place of pilgrimage for within its church exists the shrine of St. Wite, one of only two remaining intact in this country, the other being the more

Whitchurch Canonicorum

famous shrine of Edward the Confessor in Westminster Abbey. The name was altered to Candida towards the end of the Middle Ages (St. Candida's Day is 3rd October), and it is thought she could have been an Anglo-Saxon hermit who devoted her life to good causes.

The shrine, which is of local golden stone, dates from the early 13th century and is built into the wall in the north transept. The upper portion consists of a Purbeck marble tomb chest, underneath which a hollow stone contains three large oval openings. Within these openings would have been placed the injured and diseased limbs of pilgrims who had come for healing – for the marble tomb chest above contains the remains of St. Wite.

The relics were discovered in April 1900, after movement of the walls of the north transept caused an ancient 13th century crack in the tomb chest to widen. When the broken piece was removed a lead casket was discovered in the interior. Measuring 2ft.5ins long and 8 ins. high, it bore a Latin inscription which translated reads, 'Here rest the relics of St. Wite'. The contents appeared undisturbed and were believed to be the bones and teeth of a small woman aged about forty. They were returned to the tomb chest where they have remained ever since.

Today visitors to the shrine will find its floor covered with petitions placed there by folk asking for healing for themselves, their relatives or friends – the only shrine to maintain a continuous record of pilgrimage extending over one thousand years.

The shrine of St. Wite, Whitchurch

13. In and Around Weymouth

BINCOMBE

This church, situated in a peaceful small village near Upwey, is in the Early English style of c1250-1350. Features of particular interest include earlier Norman work to be seen in the blocked-up north doorway and the font, the latter bearing traces of the fittings of a former cover. There is a blocked-up hagioscope (squint) in the north wall, and a blocked-up window high up in the south wall is visible from the outside. The windows are of the mid-1400s, and the chancel arch was restored in 1862, at which time the chancel was lengthened and the floor raised.

Before the Norman Conquest 'Beincombe', as it was then known, belonged to Earl Harold, after which William the Conqueror gave it to the monastery of St. Stephen of Caen. Much later it contained a large encampment of soldiers, mainly regiments of the German Legion. The earliest church register of the church dates from 1658 and an entry for the year 1801 includes the names of two young German mercenaries of the York Hussars who deserted and were subsequently caught. Accused of spying, they were tried and shot at the crossroads, and are believed to be buried in the churchyard beneath two flat, nameless grave-stones lying side by side.

In 1570 the village was bought by Gonville and Caius College, Cambridge, who still own it and are patrons of the living. Since 1808, when the rectory was burnt down, the rector has lived at Broadwey. The parishes of Bincombe and Broadwey have been united with Upwey and Buckland Ripers since 1979.

Bincombe

UPWEY *St. Laurence*

This late 15th, early 16th century church is built of Upwey stone and dedicated to the saint who died a martyr's death and was burnt on a gridiron. The tower is tall, with a number of fearsome gargoyles and pinnacles. A small piece of wall to the rear of the

Upwey St Laurence

building is all that remains of the church which existed in the 13th to 14th centuries. Just above the porch is a water-spouting gargoyle with a boy astride a wolf holding its mouth open.

Passing through the porch and iron-studded 500 year-old door into the church, frescoes are to be seen on the inside walls to left and right. Those to the west are quotations from the Book of Proverbs, chapter 24, v20-22, though the lettering in the bottom right-hand corner is damaged and indecipherable. Of particular interest are the painted Tudor Roses between the arches of the fine north arcade. These have, in recent years, been renewed, after re-discovery beneath old wall-paint and inch-thick plaster.

Three wooden plaques displayed on the walls are believed to have been taken from the pedestal of a Jacobean pulpit. Another point of interest is the pre-Christian Green Man (or Jack-in-the-Green) situated at the top of the pillar of the north arcade nearest to the tower. The south arcade was built at a later dated (1838), and is an exact copy of the north arcade, apart from the fact that the Green Man is missing. As the latter has pagan connections it is thought that this may have been deliberate. The belfry carries six bells.

Worth noting, too, is the paler colour of the bottom ten inches or so of all of the pews. This was the result of a torrential storm which occurred in July 1955, when water swept down the valley, flooding into the church.

Just down the road is Upwey Wishing Well and tea rooms for which the village is famous.

Buckland Ripers

BUCKLAND RIPERS

This tiny village in its peaceful rural setting includes a church and a manor house. The church, in Perpendicular style, has a bell-cote, roses around the porch, and the date (of rebuilding) cut into the lintel. Both church and manor house were damaged in a mid-17th century fire, but a two-light west window, the north door behind the stove, the hexagonal font, and some walling to the west gable remain from the medieval building.

The Communion rails would appear to date from 1655, other furnishings being apparently disposed of during 19th century restoration which included varnish on pitch-pine affecting roof, pulpit, pews and panel. As stated by the late Eric Ricketts R.I.B.A. in his *The Buildings of Old Weymouth* (1977), however, *'such destruction cannot deface the intrinsic beauty of this little church, one of the most atmospheric in our beautiful hinterland'*.

This church used to be part of the Radipole benefice, until transferred to the Upwey group c1981.

RADIPOLE *St. Ann*

Here in the little village of Radipole on the river Wey, a small church, a fine manor house, and a church school (across the road) are attractively grouped together. Once the mother-church of Melcombe Regis, St. Ann's has evolved over the last 750 years and must be the oldest building in

Ancient altar in Radipole churchyard

Weymouth, part of it dating back to 1250. The school (with recently modernised interior and now put to other uses) was built in 1840 in Gothic style, its tall 'Tudor' stack being particularly striking.

Some time in the 14th century, chantry chapels (now called transepts) were added to the church, and the chancel and arch were rebuilt. In both north and south chapels (rebuilt in the 18th century) is a piscina. The medieval roof trusses and purlins remain and there is a 13th century font. The south porch was rebuilt in 1733 and the churchwarden of that time, William Mowlam, had his initials carved over the entrance. Victorian restoration work of 1862 resulted in the removal of the 15th century chancel screen, the Georgian three-decker pulpit and the box pews. A Victorian gallery replaces the original musicians' gallery which dated from Elizabethan times. The Communion table is Jacobean (see chap. 7)

Of particular interest is the Priest's door with ogee arched head in the south wall of the chancel, and the 14th century window in the north chapel. A photograph on the west wall shows the church as it appeared at the beginning of the 19th century, when access was through the yard of an adjacent farm. A striking feature of the exterior of the little church is the unique Italianate triple bell turret, thought to be 16th century. In the churchyard are many old tombs and there is a memorial to one of the young victims of the East Indiaman, *Earl of Abergavenny*.

St Ann

Interior of St Ann, Radipole

WEYMOUTH *St. Mary*

This town-situated church is of good Classical style, rebuilt c1815 by James Hamilton. It belongs to the Radipole/Melcombe Regis team ministry.

The exterior is of Portland stone ashlar and the interior has galleries on three sides painted with coats-of-arms. In times past the very tall pulpit would have enabled the preacher to be at eye-level with the galleries, which in those days would have been full of worshippers on a Sunday - as would the body of the church. In recent times, the transepts have been curtained off and are used as parish rooms.

Outstanding is the painting over the Communion table of the Last Supper by James Thornhill, Hogarth's father-in-law, at one time Member of Parliament for the Borough.

St Mary's, Weymouth

WYKE REGIS, *All Saints*

Wyke's spacious 15th century church stands 26ft above sea level looking out across Dead Man's Bay. One of the oldest buildings in the village, it has for centuries acted as both a landmark and seamark, its three large churchyards bearing silent witness to the many ships wrecked on the Chesil Beach. Consecrated in 1455 and constructed mainly of Upwey (and probably some Portland) stone, it was at one time the mother church of Weymouth where, on a fine summer's evening, its peal of eight bells is clearly audible. Around it clusters the old part of the village. There is slight evidence that a Norman church formerly stood on the site of All saints, for a corbel of much earlier date than others is believed to be Norman.

An unusual feature of this church is a room containing an irregular hagioscope and known as the 'Bones Room'. Now used as a vestry, its somewhat gruesome title derives from post-Reformation days when it was used as a depository for bones which came to the surface during the digging of graves in the churchyard. This was a not infrequent occurrence, for normal interments were limited to the south side of the church, the north side (once known as the Devil's Side), being reserved for outlaws, criminals and suicides, as well as having close associations with shipwrecks and smugglers. The resultant overcrowding of the south side led to some unavoidable disturbance, particularly as medieval graves were not more than 3ft. in depth. In 1870 the collection of bones in the Bones Room was buried in a large grave dug opposite the old rectory.

Many burials took place inside the church, too, the dead said to be lying side by side and end to end over almost the entire area of the floor. The last interment inside the church was that of Elizabeth Russell who paid £50 for the privilege.

In 1805 the wreck of the *Earl of Abergavenny*, took place with the loss of 300 lives. Amongst the dead was the poet Wordsworth's brother, John, the captain of the ship. His grave, with no stone to mark it, lies on the south side of the church.

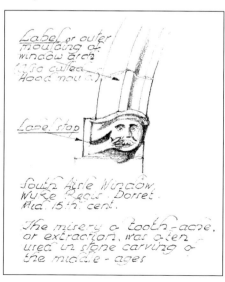

Label or outer moulding of window arch also called Hood mould

Lane stop

South Aisle Window, Wyke Regis, Dorset. Mid 15th cent.

The misery of tooth-acre, or extraction, was often used in stone carving of the middle-ages

Fleet

FLEET *Holy Trinity*

The now almost non-existent village of East Fleet possesses two churches, one of which was the parish church until ruined by a storm in 1824 when a 95-ton ship was hurled over the Chesil Bank. The village was washed away with the exception of six cottages, of which five were wiped out by fire in 1938, but have since been rebuilt. Of the church only the chancel remains, within which may be seen three tablets to the Mohun family, two dated 1603 and 1612 respectively having brasses depicting fourteen sons and sixteen daughters, children of the two couples commemorated. There is said to be an underground passageway beneath the chancel once used by smugglers.

The new parish church was built in 1827 at the expense of George Gould, the then vicar, to an attractive design by Strickland. It stands in a leafy setting amongst beech trees below the level of the road, the pinkish tinge of its brickwork a result of the lichen growing over the smooth ashlar surface. It has an apsidal sanctuary with a decorated plaster ceiling. A marble wall monument in a recess was placed there by George Gould in memory of his father and three carved figures round an urn dating from 1818 are in high relief.

ABBOTSBURY *St. Nicholas*

This church is largely 15th century and possesses an early Jacobean or late Tudor pulpit of 1638, panelled and with a high back and sounding board. Of particular interest are the two holes in the pulpit's canopy, made by the bullets of Cromwell's men when church and nearby manor were garrisoned for Charles during the Civil War. An extract from a contemporary account of the attack by Sir Ashley Cooper on 8th November 1644 still exists. *After a hot bickering,* it reads, *the church was carried and all 13 defenders taken. The manor was blown up and all within it perished.*

Abbotsbury, St Nicholas

When the timbers of the north aisle were being removed during the renovation of 1930 two more bullet holes were discovered. Located in one of the beams of the aisle roof the flattened-out bullets were found to be still fixed inside.

Over the chancel is a plaster barrel ceiling of 1638 depicting leaves and faces, human and angelic. There is a 15th century font with a modern base and some 17th and 18th century glass. The large reredos of painted wood and plaster is 18th century, and the gallery dates from 1807.

A Saxon church had existed in this attractive village in olden times, though it was the Abbey that was of prime importance. On the break-up of the monastery, the land passed to Sir Giles Strangways and has been held by his descendents, the Earls of Ilchester, ever since. Large and picturesque, its houses and cottages of yellow-brown stone, mostly thatched, Abbotsbury became important in ancient times mainly due to its association with the Benedictine monastery of St. Peter founded 900 years ago during the reign of King Canute.

Interior

Yet it is for its massive tithe barn of buttressed stone erected about five hundred years ago that Abbotsbury is famous. 276 feet long by 31 feet wide, this impressive building once formed part of the monastery and remained intact after the Dissolution. Originally used as a grain-store and for shearing sheep it is now in ruins for half its length.

PORTESHAM *St. Peter*

This pretty village lies in the shadow of Portesham Hill. Its church is of Norman origin, from which part of a blocked arcade survives. The chancel is of the 13th century with a doorway surviving from this period. The remainder of the building is of the 15th century.

With its limestone exterior the church appears almost white in the sunshine. The tower is well-built and typically Dorset in design. The remains of another tower are to be seen on its northern side. There is a font of the 13th century, a 16th century chancel screen, a Jacobean pulpit, and a 17th century Communion table. The nave has a wagon roof. The interior is Victorian and there is an unusual epitaph on the south wall referring to one, Mary Weare:

> *'Whose good meek heart did always shun*
> *Such things as ought not to be done'.*

Outside, back-to-back with it, is a table tomb with another epitaph:

> *'William Weare lies here in dust,*
> *As thou and I and all men must,*
> *Once plundered by Sabean force,*
> *Some call it war but other worse'.*

Thus the two inscriptions to the 17th century couple are divided by the church wall.

There is a scratch dial on the outside wall of the church. (see chap.20).

Portesham, St Peter

CORTON *St. Bartholomew*

Corton Chapel lies off the Friar Waddon to Portesham road and was originally built as a chantry chapel to the adjacent manor house. At the time of the Domesday Book it was owned by Roger de Curcelle and was valued at £7. At this time, too, it was referred to as 'Corfeton' meaning

Corton

'town of the gap'. (One wonders how such a remote spot could be designated a town.) Chapel and farm are situated at the bottom of a steep incline. The little chapel nestles against the hillside and the lovely old manor farmhouse stands just below. The turning is signposted but could easily be missed.

The chapel is perfectly proportioned, its interior neat and well-cared for. At Harvest time, the ancient altar (almost certainly one of very few remaining in this country) looks superb against a background of chrysanthemums, dahlias and Michaelmas daisies. Typical of its kind, it consists of a long flat slab of stone supported by two stone uprights. All the furnishings are in miniature to fit the building, including the lectern and font.

In 1552, with the passing of the Chantry Act which forbade these chapels to continue in use, it became a wheelwright's shop and at some time carpentry work took place within its walls. Later on outhouses were built onto either end and it became stabling for horses and accommodation for poultry. During the 19th century a report of the building passed to the diocese, as a result of which it was decided to restore it to its former usage. The sum of £250 was needed for its restoration, but the money was raised and the chapel re-consecrated by the Bishop of Salisbury in 1897.

Nowadays the chapel is used for a variety of services during the year, including christenings. It is always open during the daytime.

14. Portland

AVALANCHE CHURCH *St. Andrew, Southwell*

Interior of Avalanche Church

This attractive little building is a lasting memorial to those who perished on the fateful night of 11th September 1877 when two ships, the *Avalanche* and the *Forest*, collided in a Force 8 gale about 12 miles offshore south-west of Portland.

The *Avalanche* was an iron, three-masted, full-rigged clipper of 1,160 tons, on passage to Wellington, New Zealand with a crew of 34 and 63 passengers, most of the latter returning home after visiting England, the rest being emigrants. The *Forest*, so called - it was said - because it took a whole forest to build her - had 22 aboard, the captain and crew. It struck the *Avalanche* with such force that it sank in five minutes. There were only three survivors – three of the crew, including the mate, who managed to leap aboard the *Forest*.

The chancel roof resembles the upturned hull of a boat, whilst a modern window replaces a plain glass one, its varying tones of wavy blue glass representing the Seven Seas. There is a circle for each of those who perished, the inscription below reads: *And the sea gave up the dead that were in it.*

A framed colour photograph of the *Forest*, taken at her launching, was presented by a great-granddaughter of the builder of the ship, who read the lesson at a Centenary service held on Sunday, 1st July 1979.

A brass tablet lists the names and description, where known, of the passengers and crew of the *Avalanche* who perished, amongst them 18 year-old Margaret Watts of Wanganui, New Zealand. In the nave hang three flags - the New Zealand flag given by the people of Wanganui, the flag of the Shaw Savill Shipping Line who owned the *Avalanche*, and the Nova Scotia flag, donated by those connected with the *Forest*. Dedicated on 3rd July 1879, the church is built entirely of Portland stone, its seating capacity being approximately one hundred. Pulpit, lectern, font, organ, and the six chancel windows were all given in memory of lost relatives and friends.

In the churchyard is the anchor of the *Avalanche* brought up from the seabed by divers.

ST. PETER-IN-THE-GROVE

Built by convict labour in 1872, St. Peter's stands close to the Youth Custody Centre. Once the Garrison church, it contains a list of regiments which occupied the Verne Citadel. (The Verne Prison is situated not far away under a flat grass-topped hill and is flanked by a deep moat-like cutting).

The church was built entirely by convicts who carved the litany desk, stone lectern, and the pulpit taken from a large block of Portland stone. Women convicts, under the direction of a reprieved murderess, made the mosaic paving in the sanctuary, the pattern for which was taken from a painting in Rome. Mystery surrounded the death of Constance Kent's young brother, who was found murdered during the night at Rode in Somerset, and anxiety extended throughout the country. The mystery remained unsolved for years, but eventually his sister, who had meantime entered a convent, confessed to the crime and served her sentence at Portland.

St Peter-in-the-Grove, Portland

ST. GEORGE, *Easton (or* ST. GEORGE, *Reforne)*

This Portland church stands remote and bleak amongst many monuments of Portland stone, replacing a medieval church dedicated to St. Andrew which became the victim of coastal erosion. Designed by Gilbert and built in 1777 in Portland ashlar, St. George's has a western tower surmounted by a cupola and a shallow central dome. Twin pulpits face each other at the crossing and are an unusual feature. The church retains its galleries at the west end and in the transepts, as well as its box pews - those to the east of the crossing facing west and away from the chancel towards the pulpits.

The church is now in the care of The Churches Conservation Trust, as is – more unusually – the churchyard with its monuments.

St. Georges Church. Portland. Dorset.

Looking east

This fine Classical Church was designed in 1753.

The font.

Most of Wren's London churches were built in Portland stone, ferried from the Island.

15. Some More Rarities

Bible Box In past times there were few copies of the Bible available and those that existed were expensive. So they were kept in locked boxes (called *Bible Boxes*), sometimes carved, to protect them and keep them clean. In 1536 Royal Authority decreed that a Latin or an English Bible should be placed in every church in the land so that it could be read by the people. To prevent theft, the Bibles were chained to the lectern.

Cadaver

Cadaver There are not many of these around. It was a rather gruesome custom of the 15th to 17th centuries to show the deceased as a corpse lying on top of the tomb.

Chained Library These often contained valuable books which were chained so they would not be stolen. There is a *Chained Library* at Wimborne Minster, though it can only be seen by visitors when accompanied by one of the vergers. It dates from 1686 and access is from the choir vestry by way of a spiral staircase of 26 steps. The oldest book is dated 1343, and amongst other interesting volumes is a *Breeches Bible* in a glass case - so called because in Genesis, chapter 3 verse 7, the word 'breeches' is used instead of 'fig leaves'.

There are about fifty chained libraries of importance in existence. (The largest of its kind in the world is to be found in Hereford Cathedral. Its oak bookcases were made in 1611 and contain 2,000 books).

Chained library

Cresset and Cropstones Few of these stones remain. Cresset stones were flat with cup-shaped hollows which could be filled with oil and floating wicks, to give light for those on night duty in the church. Cropstones were stones gathered from the fields and, to save expense, sometimes used to face the outer walls of churches, rather than using quarried blocks.

Easter Sepulchre Always situated in the north wall of the chancel, the *Easter Sepulchre* was connected in medieval times with the Good Friday and

Easter Sunday celebrations. There is one at Tarrant Hinton (see chap. 4) of date c1530, though the best example and the most elaborate is to be seen at Hawton (Notts), and coming a close second is the one at Heckington (Lincs), the latter depicting sleeping soldiers, the three women at the tomb, and the angel, the whole surmounted by the risen Christ.

14th cent.

Easter Sepulchre
Hawton Nottinghamshire

Fire Buckets A somewhat unusual sight are the two fire buckets suspended beneath the gallery at the back of Puddletown Church (see chap. 16). They are dated 1805 and have a notice attached to them bearing the words, *'the property of the Sun Insurance Company of Bath'*. Unless so displayed, fire insurance would not, apparently, have been granted.

Before the invention of the fire engine, fires were a particular hazard, and *fire-hooks* were used to pull the burning thatch from cottage roofs. These appliances (of

Fire buckets

which there is an example in the porch at St. John the Baptist, Bere Regis – see chap. 16), were for general use in the village and were kept in the church.

Funeral Cart This was a cart for carrying the coffin. Bere Regis church has an example and – outside the county – there is an interesting one at Martock in Somerset which bears the words, *'In the world to come life everlasting'*.

Funeral cart

Green Man Should there be a carved face looking down from the capital of a pillar (he may not be very obvious), with stems and foliage coming out of his mouth, this is the pre-Christian *Green Man* or *Jack-in-the-Green.* Exeter Cathedral possesses eight Green Men, but there is one nearer at hand at Upwey, St. Laurence (see chap. 13)

Hour-glass Introduced in the 16th century, hour-glasses (identical to egg-timers but larger) were much in use during the 17th century as sermon-timers. They varied in length of time, the maximum being an hour and some recording parts of hours. Their object was defeated, however, by some preachers who - when the sand ran down - turned the glass upside down and started again! In pre-Reformation times, hour-glasses would also have been used during prayer and meditation or private readings of the Scriptures.

Approximately one-hundred stands and about twenty glasses are said to remain, including one on the pulpit of Folke, St. Lawrence (see chap. 10). They were usually attached to the pulpit by an iron bracket, or occasionally to the nearby wall. At St. John the Baptist, Spetisbury (see chap.4), an old hour-glass, once attached to the pulpit, now stands on a shelf behind.

Jesse Tree The *Jesse Tree* is a window with Christ's genealogy depicted in stained glass, or carved on the mullion. The ancestry of Christ is shown in the form of a vine springing from Jesse, the father of King David, with kings and prophets often added. Jesse Trees date from around the 14th century. In Wimborne Minster (see chap. 4), the design of the centre light of the Early English east window represents the Tree of Jesse, at the top being mother and child, and below David and Solomon. It is reputed to be 15th century and to have come from Belgium.

Leper's Squint Leprosy was a common complaint in medieval times and those unfortunate enough to catch the disease became outcasts from society. They were forbidden to touch or eat with healthy people or to enter public places, including churches. So little windows (known as *'low side windows'*) were let into the outside wall of the church, usually on the south side of the chancel, with wooden shutters to open and close them. However, some say that as lepers were not allowed in public places, these low side windows were probably used for confessions or for the ringing of the Sanctus bell.

16. In and Around Dorchester

DORCHESTER *St. Peter*

This late medieval church of the 15th century occupies a prominent position in the town. Modernised in 1857, it possesses a Norman south doorway which survived the fires of the 17th and 18th centuries. It has fine arcades and original roofs, and in the north chapel, behind the organ, is a striking 17th century monument to Sir John Williams and his wife who kneel on their canopied tomb. There is another monument in the north aisle, and in the south chapel are two Crusader effigies.

Of particular interest is a plan drawn by Thomas Hardy, who is believed to have worked on the church's restoration at the time he was articled to J. Hicks. There is a tablet to an earlier Thomas Hardy who founded the grammar school in 1569.

Dorchester, St Peter

Outside the church, prominently sited, is a memorial to William Barnes, the Dorset poet.

East Chaldon interior

15th century font with modern base, Cerne Abbas

Font, Melbury Bubb

Effigy, St Mary's, Puddletown

Moreton, St Nicholas

Hazelbury Bryan

Pyramid grave in Spetisbury churchyard

Effigy, St Mary's, Puddletown

FORDINGTON *St. George*

This large church has changed greatly over the years. Its beautiful medieval tower of the 15th century is embattled and pinnacled, and said to be one of the finest in the county. The early Norman church was without aisle until the 12th century when it was widened, and there is evidence of alterations in the west wall of the tower. During the 18th and 19th centuries the south transept was remodelled and the north aisle rebuilt. In 1907 further drastic extension took place with three more bays being added to the nave, as well as north and south aisles and a very large chancel with the Edward Chapel beyond.

There was an important Roman cemetery at Fordington, and of particular note in the church is a block of Purbeck marble found under the south porch during the last century and now sited in front of the tower. On it is a Latin inscription, the earliest known in the county – a tribute to a Roman citizen by his wife and three children.

A faithful and much loved minister of this church from 1828-1880 was the Rev. Henry Moule, who came from Wiltshire. He was a great scholar and reformer, and during the disastrous cholera outbreak of 1854 he and his wife, Mary, worked tirelessly to alleviate the suffering. They are commemorated by tablets in the entrance to the church which state that they, *'with tender and unwearied faithfulness went about doing good'*. Two of their sons became bishops, and one was a friend of Thomas Hardy.

It is said that in the cemetery adjoining the church are buried the victims of the plague and it is interesting that this ground has been closed to burials ever since. German soldiers lie here, too, their graves guarded by an impressive sculpture of a kneeling German soldier.

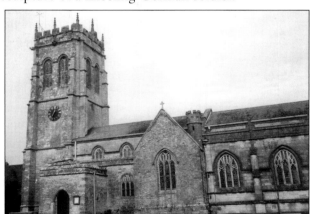

Fordington, St George

North-west
BRADFORD PEVERELL *St. Mary*

Bradford Peverell

This village is famous as the birthplace in 1698 of Dorset's well-known historian, John Hutchins, who was born at what is now known as The Old Rectory. His father was curate of the parish for many years, and his mother, who died when John was only nine, lies buried in the churchyard. The story of how, in later years, John's wife risked her life to save some valuable papers belonging to her husband, is well-known. The papers contained material collected by John over the years, the near-tragedy occurring at his last rectory at Wareham at the time the town was burned down.

St. Mary's dates from 1850, having been rebuilt at that time, and is one of few Dorset churches possessing a spire, the pale flintstone of which is hidden amongst lofty trees. Worth looking out for in the church is a medallion bearing the arms of William Wykeham who was responsible for the motto, *'Manners Makyth Man'*. In a north chancel window are some fragments of pre-Reformation glass from the previous church, and in the east window may be seen fragments of 13th and 14th century glass from New College, Oxford.

Another notable inhabitant of the village was a former vicar, Dr. Howley, who became Archbishop of Canterbury and crowned the young Queen Victoria. He was one of the two men who hastened through the night to inform the princess that King William was dead – the subject of a famous picture which hung in many Victorian homes, depicting a young girl with hair flowing loose and a shawl over her nightgown coming downstairs to meet the bearers of the news that she was Queen of England.

STRATTON *St. Mary*

This church, situated three miles or so to the north-west of Dorchester, was formerly a chapel dependent on nearby Charminster. A Norman church of the type common to village churches of that time is believed to have formerly existed here. Built c1140, long and narrow, with a roof covered with thatch

Stratton St Mary

or shingles of wood, it was replaced by an Early English (13th century) building, of which the porch, chancel arch, leper's squint and font remain.

The present church was rebuilt in 1891, though the Ham stone tower with its embattled parapet and gargoyles is of the 14th century. The original chancel was pulled down c1547. Worth noting are two Norman doorways incorporated into the nave by the restorers, some fragments of 15th century painted glass, and the upper canopy of what is thought to be a niche to hold sculpture. A tattered green and white flag bearing the red dragon of Wales hangs above the nave. According to Arthur Mee, it flew in France throughout the war and was often saluted by a native of Dorset, Edward Alexander Pope, D.S.O. His name appears on a tablet (there are several memorials to this family), along with that of another D.S.O. holder, Alan Roderick Haig-Brown.

Perhaps the church's most interesting possession is the wooden spiral staircase dating from the Tudor period, situated at the base of the tower and leading to the belfry. Narrow and enclosed in a five-sided linenfold-panelled casing of oak which rises from a pillar ending in a kind of fan tracery, it is very rare. One feels tempted to make the ascent of this unique staircase which is as old as the 15th century walls, but the narrowness – and cobwebs – deter one.

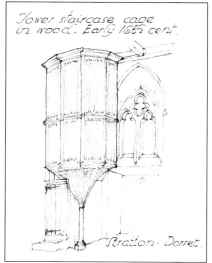

Tower staircase cage in wood. Early 16th cent.

Stratton · Dorset.

SYDLING *St. Nicholas*

St Nicholas

This interesting church, which is late Perpendicular, stands adjacent to Sydling Court, the latter built in the 1400s and formerly the seat of the Hussey family. Mainly 15th century, the church occupies the site of at least two previous buildings believed to date from earliest Christian times. The oldest part of the building is the tower which dates from 1430. Outside, a number of fine gargoyles with bodies resembling frogs, birds and apes, carry rainwater away from the roof.

As you enter by way of the north porch, note the fireplace around which, in times past, church meetings would have been held. The church's interior, which has a wagon roof, is light and airy, the medieval stained-glass windows having been destroyed in Cromwell's time, though some fragments of the original stained glass remain and have been remounted. To the right of the chancel (re-modelled in 1745 by the Smith family, then owners of Sydling Court), is a hagioscope (squint) containing a stone carving of a man's head, discovered in 1961 during repairs to the nave roof.

In the south aisle, and occasionally used, are some 18th century box pews, one having several sets of carved initials. The font, which could be the oldest item in the church, is believed to have been made from the top of a Roman pillar. Two hatchments of the Smith family, one over the south door and the other at the end of the south aisle, display their coat of arms and motto.

A clock, located in the tower and initialled ETC, is thought to have been made by a local blacksmith. Faceless, but striking the hour, it is dated 1593 and is the second oldest clock of its kind in the country, It bears the marks of hand-forging.

The bells are noted for their mellow tones. The oldest, inscribed 'Ave Maria', weighs over nineteen hundredweight and is 16th century. There is evidence that bells were cast at Sydling in the late 13th century. The organ, which is Victorian, was hand-pumped until c1978.

In the churchyard, outside the north door is a yew tree believed to be at least 500 years old. There are some interesting memorials to the south of the church, including a grave recording the death of the last miller of Sydling, marked by a millstone.

FRAMPTON *St. Mary*

This attractive village, having a park on one side containing a house built in recent years to replace an older one of 1704, lies in the heart of the Frome Valley. Originally 15th century, its church of St. Mary has been much restored and enlarged over the years, but retains a tower of 1695 built by Robert Browne. Gothic in style, with columns and buttresses, a square parapet and slender pinnacles, this tower is the church's most striking feature. The south porch was added in 1820.

The chancel was rebuilt 1747-8 and again in 1862, from which time the present pews with their unique carved candle-holders date. The south aisle was rebuilt by Benjamin Ferrey in 1871, but the chancel arch and the south arcade survive from the 15th century. Also dating from the 15th century is the octagonal stone pulpit with six carved panels, three ancient and three contemporary. It is one of only about sixty surviving in the country and is said to be one of the best. The Victorian font was given by the Duchess of Somerset in 1858. There are six bells, the oldest of which was cast in 1694.

A brass in the vestry records the fact that all the woodwork in the church was done by Thomas Campion at the time it was restored. In the north aisle are monuments and effigies to the Browne and Sheridan families of Frampton Court, benefactors of the church. An effigy to Rear Admiral Sir John Browne records that he played his part in the defeat of the Spanish Armada, and a bust of Richard Brinsley Sheridan records that he was killed in action at Cape Colony in 1901.

A plaque tells us that this village of just 300 people lost twenty-one men during the 1914-18 War.

Frampton

FROME VAUCHURCH *St. Francis*

Frome Vauchurch

In the valley of the Frome, a five minute's walk out of Maiden Newton, lies Frome Vauchurch – spelt 'Vanchurch' on some old maps. Once a much larger village, most of its dwellings have long since disappeared, but it is worth walking down the lane to see the little towerless Norman church which from 1772 to 1925 was joined to Batcombe five miles away. In 1925 the parish became united with Maiden Newton, and both now form part of the Melbury team ministry along with Toller Fratrum and Wynford Eagle. 'Vau' being Norman-French for 'val', this denotes the Frome Valley Church.

Surprisingly its dedication was unknown until quite recently, perhaps due to all its records being destroyed by fire. In March 1988, however, the little building, which is considered by some to have Saxon origins, was dedicated to St. Francis. With its thick leaning walls, narrow windows and a seating capacity of 50, it has several interesting features.

The font, for instance, is either Saxon or Norman, square topped on a round base, lead-lined, and with slightly splayed angles, while the richly carved Jacobean pulpit comprises two sides of a hexagon. Obviously much cut about, the latter does not appear to fit too well into its present position so it is thought likely that it was originally located elsewhere in the church. The nave windows are considered to be of 14th century origin, as is the porch; a 12th century doorway is now built up.

Considerable restoration took place in the 17th century and again in the 1800s, when the entirely rebuilt chancel included a narrow chancel arch with pointed head. The nave, too, appears to have been restored at this time and a new roof added c1878, when benches were introduced. There is an ancient piscina and one small bell.

The churchyard was enlarged in 1884 by land given by R.B. Sheridan, and it is sheltered by massive spreading yew trees. Two table tombs are dated 1660 and 1709.

MAIDEN NEWTON *St. Mary*

Once a market town, Maiden Newton is now a village of some three hundred houses, set amidst rolling downs and farmland. Its church, with solid central tower, dates from Norman times and stands among trees on the banks of the river Frome, within sound of water from the old mill mentioned in the Domesday Book. Much of the church dates from c1150, most of the remainder, including the tower, having been rebuilt in the 15th century.

Of particular interest is the church's ancient Norman doorway, said to be one of the oldest in the country and believed to be still hanging on its original hinges. Made in 1450, it appears never to have had a lock or latch, but the grooves in the stone-work on either side would originally have held a wooden bar for locking.

This church also has the distinction of bearing bullet holes from both Cromwellian times and from the Second World War. The latter were caused by a bullet fired from an aircraft, which penetrated a window; while Oliver Cromwell's men are believed to have fired at the building when Royalists were hiding inside – though the bullets in the ancient door have disappeared in recent times.

Of the original building, the late Norman eastern tower arch - pointed and on piers with scalloped capitals - survives. The north wall is mostly Norman and contains a Norman doorway now built up. The west wall is Norman with door and windows inserted in 1450; the south aisle and transept were added in the 14th century. There is a

Maiden Newton

low-pitched king-post roof over the nave, and behind the stone pulpit which is built into the wall is a small Norman doorway concealing a spiral staircase giving access to the ringing chamber. There are five bells, one of which dates from 1647. Two blocked doorways near the pulpit would have led to the rood loft. The font is 12th century, and there are fragments of medieval glass.

To the south of the churchyard stands the imposing former rectory, now Maiden Newton House, built in 1846 by the then rector, the Rev. the Honourable William Scott. The Scott family tombs are by the south porch.

CATTISTOCK *Ss. Peter and Paul*

Of the medieval church once existing, only the transepts remain, the rest having been rebuilt in 1855 in Early English style with an apsidal chancel by Sir Gilbert Scott. The church's most striking feature is its tall, slim, pinnacled tower of grey stone with long vertical belfry windows, which dominates the village and was added – along with the north aisle - by Scott's son, George Gilbert Scott, in 1874.

From this tower, until the Second World War, the mellow tones of a very fine carillon of thirty-five bells, cast in Louvain, would peal melodiously out over the village, attracting many folk from the neighbouring countryside. In the early 1940s, however, the bells were unfortunately destroyed by a fire in the tower (not due to enemy action), and were replaced by a modern peal of eight bells. At one time an enormous clock face spread across the tower's width, though this was later replaced by the present clock which is of smaller proportions. To appreciate the full height of the tower, one needs to view it from the south-west.

The church's interior is rich but somewhat dark and sombre, with colourful stained glass. And here is another striking feature - an elaborate and enormously tall wooden font cover in the shape of a spire, which rises to a height of 20ft. and almost touches the roof. Situated beneath the tower, it stands within a chapel having mural decorations of dark purple, greens and reds.

According to Hutchins, the west end of the church and tower were, in the 18th century, ivy-covered ruins. The new tower was apparently inspired by that of Charminster church, near Dorchester. Going further back in time, it is believed that a church certainly existed here during the Saxon period, though no evidence of it remains.

Ss. Peter and Paul

Toller Fratrum

TOLLER FRATRUM *Basil the Great*

This tiny settlement stands on a hillside overlooking the point where the river Hooke meets the river Frome. The name means 'a stream in a valley of the brethren' and refers to the Knights Hospitallers of St. John of Jerusalem who had associations with Forde Abbey.

The church stands in a very small churchyard, to the side of a long thatched barn which in turn stands at right-angles to Little Toller Farm. Possessing neither tower nor spire but only a bell turret, this church is one of only four ecclesiastical buildings in this country dedicated to Basil the Great who was one of the most important saints in the churches of the east. It was rebuilt in the early part of the 19th century and has a Norman chancel and nave.

A feature of particular note inside the church is the tub-shaped font said to be very early Norman or even Saxon. It is decorated with a number of crudely-carved figures.

TOLLER PORCORUM *St. Andrew and St. Peter*

Toller Porcorum

This attractive church comes within the Beaminster area team ministry and stands on an elevation at the centre of the village between the railway and stream. The parish registers exist up to 1615 and record an incumbent of 1235.

Inside, a Victorian iron staircase leads to the bell-ringers gallery and a spiral stone stair gives access to the bell-chamber at the top of the 15th century tower. There have been a number of alterations over the years, the high box-pews having been removed during restoration work in 1894, as was the gallery which once extended along the back and up the south side, access to which was by means of an outside wooden staircase. The ancient font is said to have been part of a Roman altar. Fine views are obtainable from the wide, clear glass windows in the south aisle.

The collapse of a length of the wall bounding the churchyard above School Lane led to an interesting discovery. Stones about two-and-a-half feet by two feet came to light, and this would seem to confirm the belief that at one time Toller Porcorum churchyard may have been a Llan or Lan, a word meaning 'holy place' – these sites, roughly circular in shape and marked out by a ring of standing stones, being created by the Celts in pre-Roman times. It would seem that there are in existence in the West Country a number of such sites which were taken over by the first Christians who built their churches in the centre of them. The stones may be seen at the east entrance to Toller Porcorum churchyard.

The village derives its name from '*toller*' meaning a stream in a valley, and '*porcorum*' (pig). Originally it was called Swynestolre or Hogstolre, and here kings hunted wild boar.

WYNFORD EAGLE *St. Lawrence*

This church was rebuilt in 1842 but a larger one once existed, situated in the water meadow to the south of the present building, on the south side of the stream close to Broadwater Cottage.

A curious feature here is a tympanum of the 12th century set in the outside of the west wall on the north side of the porch, at about seven feet above ground level. Carved in stone, it is believed to have once formed the head of the doorway of the former building. It is intact and depicts two winged dragons in angry confrontation.

This is a very small village with an unusually gabled manor house dating from 1630 and built of Ham Hill stone. Thomas Sydenham purchased Wynford in 1545 and the house was re-built in 1630 by his grandson William Sydenham. Born in the manor house in 1624 was Thomas Sydenham, who became one of London's leading physicians and is notable for having introduced quinine as a cure for the plague.

An eagle surmounts the central gable of the porch, from whence it looks out over the rolling open valley. In Norman times it formed part of a large estate held of the 'Honour of the Eagle', which the Norman Gilbert de Aquila ruled from his castle at Pevensey.

Wynford Eagle

Compton Valence

COMPTON VALENCE *St. Thomas of Canterbury*

The architect of this attractive early Victorian church was Benjamin Ferrey who rebuilt it in 1838 in Portland and Ham Hill stone, while retaining the 15th century tower. A north aisle was added at this time and the nave lengthened, while the chancel was reconstructed and vaulted in apsidal form. Unusually, the pulpit of Bath stone is not a separate piece of furniture, but is built into the wall.

A wooden Communion table replaces a former altar of Caen stone, and there are contemporary pews, their ends decorated with fleur-de-lys. The four bells in the tower are dated 1620, but were re-cast in 1870. In 1979 the 19th century clock was electrified.

A note in the porch states that in commemoration of H.M. the Queen's Coronation, her subjects in the village of Compton Valence planted trees in the churchyard, which included a golden yew and winter cherries.

This church, which stands elevated above the road and is approached by steps, belongs - along with Martinstown, Winterborne Abbas and Winterborne Steepleton - to the Winterborne Valley benefice. It lies close to the Dorchester to Bridport road in an area where mounds once existed, marking the site of an ancient British village. It is kept locked nowadays, though the key is obtainable via a telephone number supplied.

North-east

PUDDLETOWN *St. Mary*

This magnificent church, probably more than any other in Dorset, has been left unchanged – apart from the lighting – over the centuries. Mainly late medieval, there is a 15th century roof over the nave panelled in oak, the chancel dates from c1910, and there are 17th and 18th century painted texts on the walls. The embattled tower has a turret staircase on the south side.

It is, however, the 17th century fittings of this fascinating building which are of particular interest. These comprise a two-decker pulpit (consisting of canopied pulpit and prayer-desk combined) dating from 1635, high oak box pews (the seating is made up entirely of these), and a large west gallery, all dating from the mid-17th century. The gallery contains choir-stalls indented with numerous initials, presumably of choristers. According to a list of choir members, numbers stood at 26 in the 1920s.

A tumbler-shaped Norman font of the 11th century, carved with interlaced foliage, has a 17th century cover over it, placed there to comply with a direction of Archbishop Laud. The three-sided Communion rails are of the 18th century; and there is good heraldic glass in the chapel. The steps to the rood-loft are in a very good state of preservation.

In the south chapel (which resembles a museum) are many tombs and memorials to the Martyn family of two nearby manorial houses, Athelhampton and Waterston. Some of the monuments are medieval, some of later date.

A ring in the middle of the heavy oak south door is thought to have been a Sanctuary Ring.

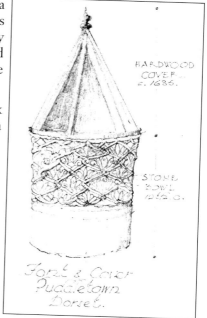

Font and cover

PIDDLEHINTON *St. Mary*

This grey stone village possesses a massive church of the 15th century, though dedicated in the 13th. Low and square, it is mostly Perpendicular in style, with large gargoyles projecting from the four corners of the tower and a mass dial on one of its buttresses. Set in a hollow and surrounded by a fair-sized graveyard, it contains many intriguing features.

Piddlehinton

In the chancel is an amusing portrait in brass of an earlier rector, Thomas Browne (1590-1617), depicted with a beard, wearing a tall hat and carrying a walking stick. Here, too, is a small priest's door and two hagioscopes (squints), along with memorials to other early rectors. A sedilia of the 15th century (under a single canopy) and comprising three stone seats would have provided cramped accommodation for priest, deacon and sub-deacon. The chancel walls have been stripped and reveal flint and stone banding. On either side are squints, and the walls and floor of the chancel are out of true and lean to the right – a phenomenon known as a 'weeping chancel' and said by some to represent the way in which the head of Christ rested when on the Cross.

Of particular interest is the turret clock at the rear of church, very rare and discovered only as recently as 1975 in the room under the bell chamber of the tower. Up to this time it had been looked upon as just a heap of old iron bars. Made by Lawrence Boyce of Puddletown in 1730 and restored in recent years, this remarkable time-piece needed to be wound every day, for which service the clerk received the sum of 6/- per annum. Having no face, the time was produced by means of a bell, the time-keeping needing to be adjusted now and again to keep in line with the sundial.

The village was once known as Hyne-Puddle (from the old English 'pidele' – marsh or fen) - meaning the 'Marsh of the Monks'. It later became Honey Puddle. In 1972 it was joined with the other valley parishes of Piddletrenthide, Plush and Alton Pancras into a single team ministry.

PIDDLETRENTHIDE *All Saints*

This massive church, with its spacious, airy interior, situated near the north boundary of the parish, has been described as one of Dorset's finest. Of Norman origin, it is mostly of the 15th century, its exterior attractively toned in shades of grey, brown, and dark yellow sandstone. The fine, graceful 15th century tower with its alarming gargoyles, has slender buttresses (on one of which is a sundial) which become pinnacles above the battlements. Along with those of Dorchester, St. Peter and Fordington St. George, this tower belongs to a small group of Dorset towers known as the 'Dorchester Group', The porch is banded with stone and flint, and the south doorway, above which are more gargoyles, is Norman - as are the piers of the chancel arch.

There is much of interest inside the church including, near the south door, a font with a base of Ham Hill stone dating from the 14th century, having an oak cover of the 17th century. In the chancel, under a single (not a triple) canopy is a sedilia, and there are hagioscopes on either side of the chancel arch. An old turret clock is to be seen at the west end of the nave, and there are hatchments around the walls, and various monuments to the Bridge family, John Bridge being notable as a silversmith who lived in the village during the 19th century.

Another well-known inhabitant of the village, born there in 1901 and buried in the churchyard, was Ralph Wightman, author and broadcaster.

Along with Piddlehinton, Hilton, Cheselbourne, Alton Pancras and Melcombe Horsey, Piddletrenthide belongs to the Piddle Valley group of churches.

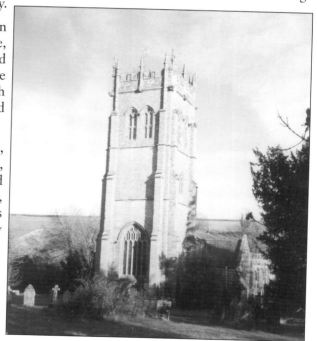

Piddletrenthide

CHESELBOURNE *St. Martin*

St Martin

This church dates from 1295 and stands isolated on a slope, surrounded on three sides by fields. The land on which it was built would have needed considerable levelling, involving much manpower.

It is thought that this spot may have been chosen because the churchyard abuts on what is believed to be a very old track leading to a large area of Celtic fields. There are apparently few ecclesiastical buildings in Dorset with so many early records; the site is said to have been used in worship for almost one thousand years.

The 500 year-old tower is pinnacled, with gargoyles, and appears tall for the length of the building. It is of two types of stone, the upper half having been added at a later date. The bells were re-hung in 1981 and there are four ancient clappers suspended on the south wall. In the bell chamber is a 17th century chest with one lock missing, along with an old oak and elm staircase which fails to reach down to the ground.

The church's interior is simple, the pillars and arches all of different shapes and sizes, due to having been built at different times. Apparently the church was not, as in the case of many others in Dorset, restored at any particular period – a fact which would seem to render it unique.

There are two hagioscopes, piscinae and a damaged water stoup. In the north wall, two small 'putti' or stone plinths date from the 16th century and are known as the 'Cheselbourne Boys', though in his *Dorset*, Arthur Mee describes them as *'two dwarfs with shields'*. The curious carving near the font he refers to as *a comical stone face crowned with a double fool's cap*, though the church guide states that the corbel supporting an arch depicts a lady with a head-dress dating from the earlier church of c1250.

A pit is believed to have existed at the east end of the churchyard, in which are said to be buried hundreds of victims of the plague. A table tomb by the main door is thought to have been used as a dole table. Worth noting are the sundials, one dated 1631 and an earlier scratch dial.

CERNE ABBAS *St. Mary*

Built of slate and Ham Hill stone, this mainly 15th/early 16th century church is situated close to the remains of the Benedictine abbey. It possesses a magnificent golden-stoned tower dating from c1500, and the interior is spacious and light with a large east window. Under a once-ancient timber roof, recently renewed, are fine panelled tower arches, and there is a medieval stone chancel screen. The Communion rails extend across the width of the sanctuary.

On a Jacobean pulpit with sounding board (a double-decker in the 19th century) may be seen the date 1640. There are some 14th century frescoes and a 15th century font with a modern base. The original box-pews (infected with dry rot) have been replaced by modern seating.

On leaving the church one should not neglect to view the gargoyles – grotesque yet splendid – on the tower. The timber-framed houses across the road probably belonged to the abbey.

Interior of St Mary

MAPPOWDER
Ss. Peter and Paul

This is a long, narrow, triangular-shaped parish of 1,900 acres. Mappowder now unites with the neighbouring parishes of Hazelbury Bryan, Stoke Wake, and Fifehead Nevill to form a team ministry.

Ss. Peter and Paul

The church is neat and tidy in appearance both outside and in. Outside it is adorned with the usual gargoyles and a flying buttress; inside the 15th century windows of clear glass give a light and airy appearance to the building. There is a modern chancel and a Norman font. The earliest records show William de Lenttom as rector in the year 1251, though the original date of the church is unknown.

Of particular interest is a small military effigy about eighteen inches in length, set in a recess in the south wall. There has been much speculation over this effigy. It is believed to be the figure of a knight who died on crusade, though his name and date of death are not known. Was his heart alone brought back for burial? And is it just his heart that is buried here? (It has been suggested that he is holding his heart in his hands).

Two sculptured heads appear on either side of the recess, believed to be an old piscina. They would seem to have been carved at dates about 200 years apart and are thought to have been taken from the old corbel table which would have extended around the chancel of the 12th century church. They were probably placed in their present position at the restoration. The tower and arcade of the south aisle are mid-15th century and there are the remains of steps to the rood-loft which are most likely of the same date. The ornately carved corbel at the head of the eastern respond of the chancel would have supported one end of the rood-loft when it existed.

To the rear of the church exists a large old building, formerly the rectory. In the wall dividing it from the churchyard may be seen a bricked-in arched doorway which at one time provided access for the parson.

MILTON ABBAS *The Abbey Church (known as Milton Abbey)*

This splendid building dates from the 14th and 15th centuries and is remarkable for its considerable height in relation to its length - for it has no nave, the Dissolution occurring before this was begun.

A church connected with a Benedictine abbey was founded here c934 by King Athelstan, but was burned down in 1309 when the wooden spire was struck by lightning. Rebuilt over the next two hundred years, it became an abbey - and later parochial, though its congregation disappeared when Squire Joseph Damer, Earl of Dorchester, destroyed the village and the grammar school to preserve his privacy, and built for himself, out of the domestic buildings of the Abbey, a mansion close by. The village - which he re-located where he could not see it - is today Dorset's showpiece, its almost identical pairs of cottages with neat gardens evenly spaced on either side of the wide street. In recent times serving as a faith-healing centre, the mansion which he built now houses the county's fourth independent public school for boys.

The Abbey possesses, amongst a number of other fine features, a reredos of 1493, a sedilia with a canopy of c1400, a Jesse window of 1849 in the south transept, some pre-Reformation glass, a modern carved oak pulpit, and 15th century windows. There is an altar tomb of date 1561 to Sir John Tregonwell, lawyer, who obtained the Abbey for £1,000, and a monument to a descendant, (also named John Tregonwell - and the founder of Bournemouth), which records his *thankful acknowledgment of God's wonderful Mercy in his preservation when he fell from the top of this Church.* As a five-year-old he had leant too far over the parapet of the building to pick a wild rose and parachuted down on his stiff nankeen petticoats, whereupon he began to pick daisies.

The Abbey stands in a peaceful, solitary setting in a valley surrounded by hills, a good view of it being obtainable from along the road leading to Hilton. In the grounds, 111 turfed steps lead up to the little chapel of St. Catherine on the Hill with its Norman walls, windows and door.

Milton Abbas

BERE REGIS
St. John the Baptist

This church of Saxon origin is said to be one of the loveliest in the country and contains much of interest. Largely rebuilt in the 12th century and altered and enlarged in medieval times, it was restored in the 19th century by G.E. Street. The spire is of flint and stone and the external walls are of stone and flint and brick banding.

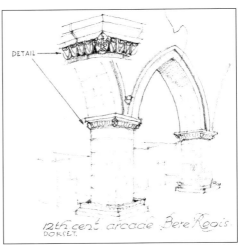

DETAIL

12th cent arcade Bere Regis DORSET.

The nave arcades with their pointed arches are in Transitional Norman style, the pillars having richly carved capitals. Twelve almost life-size figures project from the trusses on either side of the magnificent carved and painted oak mock-hammerbeam roof. They are unique and were given by Cardinal Morton, Henry VIII's chancellor and patron of the living, who was born in the parish of Milborne St. Andrew. A theory exists that they are in alphabetical order, starting with Andrew on the northern side and finishing up with Thomas on the south.

The font is Norman and there is some 16th century oak seating with carved ends. In the south aisle, the Turberville monuments of Purbeck marble are also 16th century, the Turberville family being the inspiration for Thomas Hardy's novel, *Tess of the D'Urbervilles*. In the south aisle is a chapel to the T'urberville family, and in the north aisle is the Morton chantry, the archbishop's parents being buried beneath its raised floor. Not to be missed are the many angels covering the chancel roof.

Carved on the arches cut into the south wall of the nave, and apparently intended as a warning against the deadly sins of gluttony and drunkenness, is the man with the toothache clutching his jaw, and the man with the headache grasping his forehead. Such afflictions must have presented a major problem to those living in the Middle Ages. Another feature of interest is the funeral cart in the north aisle.

On leaving this remarkable old church which is mentioned in the Domesday Book, one should note in the porch the fire hooks for removing thatch from burning roofs. The churchyard is peaceful and contains a number of yew trees.

AFFPUDDLE *St. Lawrence*

This mainly Perpendicular church of pale grey chequered stone and flint dates from the 13th century (from which a doorway survives), and was enlarged in the 15th century. It has a 15th century tower with golden stone pinnacles, and stands in a peaceful churchyard containing a number of large yew trees, amid the perpetual background sound of running water - for the river Piddle runs nearby. Arthur Mee describes this village of thatch brick and stone as *the most lovable in Dorset*.

Inside the church, the chancel is Early English, with a Norman font. Pew and bench ends are carved with linenfold and floral patterns, made in 1547 by a former vicar, Thomas Lyllyngton, as was the oak pulpit. Stairs lead to a rood-loft, and there is a holy water stoup, a piscina, and two Norman fonts, one of which was brought from nearby Holy Trinity, Turners Puddle, now redundant.

Affpuddle shares its church with nearby Briantspuddle which does not possess one of its own.

St Lawrence

17. In and Around Dorchester

South-east
STINSFORD *St. Michael*

Stinsford Church

Of 13th century origin, this church (Thomas Hardy referred to it as Melstock in his *Under the Greenwood Tree*) possesses a 13th century chancel arch and south arcade. Largely rebuilt in the 18th century and rebuilt again in 1883 by J. Hicks, little remains of the original, though the tower dates from the 14th century and there is a 13th century font with arcading. On the tower is a little stone figure - a Saxon carving of St. Michael with wings, long robes and sandals. Still remaining, too, is the simple chancel arch, the stairway to the rood-loft, and a piscina.

It was to this church that the Hardy family came Sunday by Sunday – Thomas's grandfather, father and uncle - for more than 40 years, carrying fiddles and a cello to form the church orchestra of which they were the leading members. The musician's gallery, at the rear of the building which they occupied, ceased to exist for many years but has recently been rebuilt.

In the peaceful little churchyard are the graves of several members of the Hardy family, including that of the novelist whose heart lies buried with his first wife, Emma Lavinia Gifford (whom he married in 1874), though his ashes are in Westminster Abbey; also of his second wife, Florence Dugdale, who survived him by nine years. There is a memorial window to Thomas Hardy in the church, dedicated by Bishop Jocelyn in November 1931.

WEST STAFFORD *St. Andrew*

Restored in 1895, at which time the chancel was added, this church lying in the Frome valley has an interesting interior. It is aisleless (i.e. with no side aisles), with a south porch and west tower partially rebuilt in 1640 but originally of the 15th century. The chancel was added c1898.

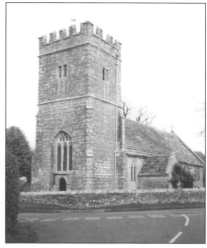

St Andrew's

Over the nave and chancel are plastered low-pitched wagon roofs and there is a west gallery with the royal arms of James I. The furnishings are particularly noteworthy and include a studded door to the oak Communion rails, and oak pews with simply carved panels. There is a pulpit with a sounding board, and the chancel screen incorporates the reading desk.

The east window has colourful Victorian glass depicting Christ, a group of red-winged angels worshipping, and the disciples. There is an alabaster effigy of Canon Southwell Smith (1898) in the north wall of the chancel - rector of the church for 60 years, throughout almost all of the Victorian era. A second benefactor, a member of the Gould family, gave the brass chandelier and candle brackets, and there is a commemoration tablet on the north wall of the nave.

Near to the church are a tithe barn and the old rectory. The former is buttressed and thatched, the latter has an unusual Jacobean fireplace and an old desk at which Wordsworth used to sit and write his poems.

WHITCOMBE *(dedication unknown)*

Whitcombe

Situated in a hollow in a field beside the Dorchester to Broadmayne road where it has stood for centuries, this church is small and ancient with a 15th century tower, its foundations one thousand years old. Its interior is simple, light and yellow-washed, with parquet flooring and oil lamps, an Early English chancel and a narrow 13th century nave. Apart from its Norman font, it is completely devoid of furniture. There are the remains of what is believed to be a Saxon cross, and in a chancel window are two glass fragments, a white rose and a yellow sun, which have existed there for five hundred years. On the north wall is a mural which probably belongs to the 14th century and depicts St. Christopher carrying the Christ Child. The triplet lancet windows are 15th century, as is the old grey tower, and there is a blocked-up north door.

Outside, the limestone of the building and the wall surrounding it gleam white against the grass. The church has no dedication and possesses no rectory. It has no income, being held in plurality with the neighbouring church at Winterbourne Came, and is now in the care of The Churches Conservation Trust. A service is held here just once a year – usually during August – on which occasion the congregation are asked to bring their own chairs.

Apart from its great antiquity, Whitcombe's more recent claim to fame lies in its connection with Dorset's famous cleric / schoolmaster / poet, William Barnes, in whose memory it has been preserved since 1912, there being a plaque to this effect inside the church. First as curate and then as rector of nearby Winterbourne Came, Barnes preached his first and last sermon (in 1885) at Whitcombe. Farther along the road may be seen the rectory of Came where he lived and where he died in 1886.

Blocked up doorway at Whitcombe

WINTERBORNE CAME *St. Peter*

This small church, almost hidden behind garden walls, stands in the grounds of 18th century Came House. Mainly of the 15th century, the upper part of the tower was added in the early 1600s.

The interior, which was refurnished in Victorian times, contains a fine early 16th century screen with an inscription in black lettering which reads: *Let us hear the conclusion of all things. Fear God and keep his commandments for that touches all men if God judges all things.* The panelled Jacobean pulpit is 17th century and there is an ancient font, some 16th century hatchments, some mid-Victorian glass, and a modern carved lectern with the figure of St. Peter holding a key.

Double table-tomb effigies in the chancel are to John Meller and his wife of Shakespearian times, together with their five sons and two daughters, kneeling. Of the two memorials, one is to Colonel Dawson-Damer, an earl's son who had two horses shot from under him at Waterloo; the other to a kinsman of his, Seymour Dawson-Damer, who died in the First World War.

William Barnes, the Dorset poet, was rector here, as well as of nearby Whitcombe. He lies buried in a simple grave beneath the church wall.

The church is now cared for by The Churches Conservation Trust – 'a consecrated building – a part of English history maintained for the benefit of this and future generations'.

St Peter's

WEST KNIGHTON *St. Peter*

St Peter's

This peaceful rural village lying three miles from Dorchester is mentioned in the Domesday Book. It stands just off the heath and the Broadmayne road and covers quite a large area surrounding the village of Broadmayne on three sides.

The small 12th century church, of which the chancel with its Norman arch is the oldest part, belongs to the Watercombe benefice. It was tastefully restored by Thomas Hardy in 1899, at which time the building was extended and the roof lowered. When the ceiling was removed the discovery was made of a circular painting high up on the east wall of the nave. A large gallery, benches, and three box-pews of the Victorian era are all of pine, and there are two hagioscopes. A wall-painting of the Lord's Prayer is partially obliterated by a monument.

Also in the church are brass plates to the memory of the Hawkins family who lived at Lewell Lodge, and in the churchyard with its several large yew trees is the grave of the Chilcotts, also of Lewell Lodge. Here, too, is a table tomb of John Trenchard.

Interestingly, it is thought that a bell in the tower may have rung out the death of Queen Elizabeth I.

Originally this village was known as Chenistetone, meaning 'place of the lesser nobles or knights', which in due course became Cnititon, Knieteton, Knittetone and Knyghteton. In 1795 the two livings, Broadmayne and West Knighton, were united, and in 1977 the benefice was joined with the other three parishes, Owermoigne, Warmwell and Holworth. The present population of the village is 253.

WARMWELL *Holy Trinity*

The village of Warmwell lies just off the Dorchester to Wool road, beyond the Warmwell crossroads. One of five parishes in the Watercombe benefice, its 700 year-old church is Perpendicular in style with a substantial 15th century square tower. It was restored in 1881 at which time the chancel was rebuilt, and inside is to be found a Norman font with an octagonal bowl carved all round with arches.

During the Second World War an aerodrome existed on the adjacent heathland where fighter aircraft refuelled before crossing the channel. In the churchyard are many tombstones of German and Italian prisoners of war who worked here, and of R.A.F. fighter pilots who died during the war.

The village possesses a fine 17th century manor house.

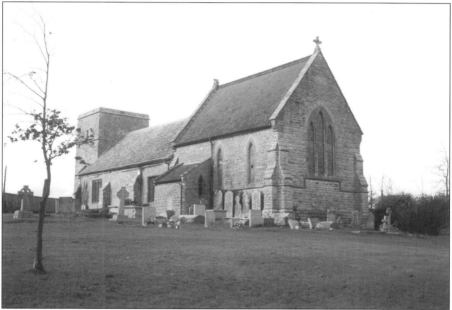

Warmwell, Holy Trinity

OWERMOIGNE *St. Michael*

St Michael's

Lying just north of the Dorchester to Wareham road and three miles from Ringstead Bay, the village of Owermoigne has been described by Arthur Mee as *a charming village of tall trees and thatched cottages.* Said to be much older than its church, it is one of five parishes united in a single team ministry, (the others being Broadmayne, Warmwell, West Knighton and Holworth), and has altered out of all recognition in the last sixty years. Modern houses and bungalows are much in evidence though there is still some thatch, and the centre around the church remains unspoilt. It takes its name from Ralph Moyne who held the manor of Oweres (originally a Saxon settlement known as Ogre in the Hundred of Winfrith) in the reign of Edward I.

The church, originally Norman but rebuilt in 1883, is small and Gothic in style with an old battlemented tower, and still retains some of the original Norman building. The first recorded rector was Walter Chaundos, instituted on 15th May 1333 under the patronage of John Le Moigne. Worth noting is a board in the south wall giving details of the Adam Jones Charity set up in 1653, which is still being administered by a board of trustees to help needy cases in the village.

Amongst the brass plates is one on the south wall of the chancel to John Sturton (1506), who lived in the manor. Another, to 'Nicholas Cheverell deceased Jan MVCXLVIII', has disappeared, along with a church chest dating from 1625, and a chalice and paten.

The church records are reputed to be the best kept in the diocese of Salisbury and are complete from 1596. Amongst them are a number of entries relating to Thomas Hardy's ancestors, members of the Hardy family having lived in the village from 1664 to 1793.

EAST CHALDON (or Chaldon Herring) *St. Nicholas*

This well-kept church stands in a peaceful setting a short way back from the road. Norman in origin and with a rare Saxon font discovered in a farmyard in 1897, it was restored in the 15th century and again in 1879. The Communion table, pulpit and lectern were made by a canon of Upwey with his own hands. The rare Saxon font was discovered in a farmyard in 1897. In the well-tended churchyard may be seen the tombstone of Elizabeth Muntz, the sculptress, which was designed by herself before her death.

The village lies remote amongst the downs nine miles west of Wareham. To the rear and above rises the ridge known as Fossil Hill from which marvellous views of the surrounding countryside are obtainable and where a series of rounded barrows known as the Five Marys (or Meers) is to be found.

At intervals along the nearby cliffs are three marker stones in the form of sculptured whelk shells set in stone niches each at a different angle. They are monuments to the three Powys brothers – John Cowper Powys, novelist, A.R. Powys, architect and secretary to the Society for the Protection of Ancient Buildings (see chapter 4, Winterborne Tomson), and T.F. Powys, novelist, who lived at East Chaldon in a small red Victorian house called 'Beth Car'. Between village and sea, a memorial stone to Llewellyn Powys bears the dates '13th Aug 1884 to 2nd Dec. 1939', and the words, *The Living, The living, He shall praise Thee.*

Chaldon Herring is named in the Domesday Book, as is neighbouring West Chaldon, formerly known as Chaldon Boys. Until 1446 both had their own parish churches, though they were subsequently united and by 1460 nothing was left of Chaldon Boys except the chancel.

The name 'Chaldon' derives from Chavedon, i.e. 'the hill were calves were pastured', or 'the hiding down place'. 'Herring' refers to a Norman family of the name 'Harang' whose coat of arms bears three herrings.

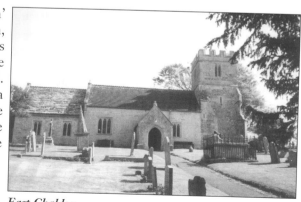

East Chaldon

St Nicholas Church

MORETON *St. Nicholas*

This church was damaged by bombs in 1940, part of the north wall being demolished and not properly rebuilt until 1950. Also destroyed were all the stained-glass widows, which were later replaced by fine engraved glass by Laurence Whistler, for which the little building is now famous.

Rebuilt in 1776 in early Gothic revival style by James Frampton of Moreton House, it stands in a circular churchyard believed to be a pre-Christian religious site. The north aisle was added in 1841. The chancel is apsidal and has plaster vaulting as does the nave. Of the five engraved apse windows by Whistler (1950), described as 'a celebration of spiritual light', the three engravings of a fishing boat, harvest and the bombed church are particularly lovely. Also to be seen are some 18th and 19th century monuments to the Frampton family.

T.E. Lawrence (Lawrence of Arabia), who met his untimely death in 1935 whilst riding his motor-cycle along nearby lanes, is buried in the cemetery 200 yards out of the village. Included amongst the mourners at his funeral service in the little church was Sir Winston Churchill.

South-west:

WINTERBOURNE ST. MARTIN (MARTINSTOWN)

This 15th century church, (more familiarly known as Martinstown), underwent considerable restoration from 1895 to 1907. It is mainly Perpendicular with a good tower, and possesses a Norman font with a square bowl decorated with arches, a Jacobean pulpit, and a silver chalice dating from Elizabethan times.

In 1947 five new bells were hung as a memorial to those who died in the Second World War, replacing an earlier peal sold to defray expenses and which had been silent for many years.

In springtime this attractive village is remarkable for its wonderful display of daffodils. A stream (the Winterbourne) flows between the houses and the road, and is spanned by bridges to some of the stone-tiled or thatched houses and cottages, a number of which have stone porches. The surrounding countryside is rich in grass-covered barrows.

Martinstown was once famous for its church band, these groups being popular from the end of the 18th century until the end of the 19th. The Martinstown group consisted of four clarinets, a hautboy (played by a mason) and a base-viol. The last Dorset church band ceased playing c1895.

Martinstown

WINTERBOURNE STEEPLETON *St. Michael and All Angels*

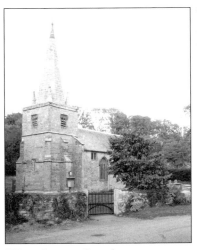

Winterbourne Steepleton

This ancient church is of Saxon origin, but dates mainly from the 13th century, only the quoins (corner stones) at three corners of the nave remaining from the original building. The short stone steeple topping the low west 14th century tower is probably 18th century; the south porch and the doorway, with a Norman arch, are 14th and 12th century resectively. The main door is late 17th century/early 18th, and the windows are 15th century. The nave and font are Norman. The north doorway was blocked up in the 17th century, and can best be seen from the churchyard. At the west end is a white-painted minstrel's gallery of 1708.

The north wall-paintings in the nave are of particular interest. Prior to 2002 they were in a state of considerable deterioration. Since then the interior of the church has undergone redecoration, the twelve areas of wall-paintings which cover seven different periods of the 13th, 15th, 16th and 17th centuries having been restored. These include a fragment of text of a style earlier than others in the church, and there is also one half of a Stuart coat of arms, and a 15th century fragment of St. Christopher partially covering some 16th century lettering of a portion of the Creed.

Originally carved on an outside wall of the nave, but now re-sited in the chancel is a stone angel. Bound with chains he looks back towards his raised feet and fluttering garments and is believed to be St. Michael or an angel cast out of Heaven. The 'flying angel', as he is known, dates from the 11th or 12th centuries and is an outstanding example of Saxon sculpture thought to be pre-Conquest.

In the churchyard are a number of ancient table tombs, some with gargoyles and skull and crossbones. Near the porch is the stone socket of a medieval cross, and on the south wall is a scratch dial probably dating from the 14th century.

Outside the road winds between trees and a stream flows past thatched, flint-built cottages in a peaceful and picturesque setting.

LITTLE BREDY *St. Michael and All Angels*

This is a tranquil spot, cut off from the outside world. The name of the village derives from a Celtic word meaning 'to boil or throb' – a reference to the little stream that has risen here for more than 2,000 years. The modern pronunciation of 'Bredy' is said to be misleading; people with their roots in the valley still say 'Briddy' which is apparently nearer the sound of the original name.

A path leads down a slope to a little church half-hidden by beech trees and with an unusual and distinctive-looking spire. On entering one discovers that whilst some older parts of the building were partially incorporated, including the original late 13th century chancel and 14th century tower, it dates mostly from 1850, at which time it was rebuilt by Robert Williams of Bridehead to the design of Benjamin Ferrey. It was at this time that the spire was added.

Bridehead House (c1830) and grounds lie below the church.

St Michael and All Angels

PUNCKNOWLE *St. Mary*

This village (pronounced 'Punnell') possesses many attractive thatched cottages. The Crown Inn stands opposite the church, adjacent to which is a charming 16th century manor house. The church is Norman in origin and its squat tower is 12th century reconstructed in the 17th century.

Inside the church are a number of monuments to the Napier, Napper, or Naper family. The largest, dated 1691 and situated in the north aisle, commemorates Sir Robert Napier. It includes the helmet which once carried the Napier crest, gauntlet and spurs of the early 17th century - until these were stolen in 1975. Another, having initials only, commemorates Sir Robert Napier who was the High Sheriff of the county and died in 1700. The inscription runs:

> '*Reader, when as thou hast done all thou can'st, thou art but an unprofitable servant. Therefore this marble affords no roome for fulsome flattery or vaine praise Sr. R.N.*'

The north aisle was added in 1891 though the nave is modern. In the south aisle is the Bexington Chapel, used as a vestry since 1966 and containing an undated memorial to William Napier.
There are two fonts from the 12th century.

Interior of St Mary's

SWYRE *Holy Trinity*

This small grey village lies in a valley running down to the Chesil Beach. The church is a plain, unadorned little building dating from 1505, though only the tower and chancel arch remain from this period, it having been largely rebuilt in 1863. Its list of

Holy Trinity

rectors dates back to John de Candel of 1297, no previous records surviving. The Dorset historian, John Hutchins, is amongst their number, he having been instituted to the living in 1729. He is noted as having repaired the chancel at his own expense.

Some early 16th century brasses commemorate the Russell family of Berwick House a mile to the north. John Russell rose from farmer's son to courtier in 1506, when a ship with the daughter of the King and Queen of Castille aboard, together with her husband, Philip, Archduke of Austria, had been forced to put into Weymouth due to bad weather. The royal couple were entertained by Sir John Trenchard at Wolfeton House, near Dorchester, and because John Russell could speak Spanish, he was called upon to act as interpreter. He accompanied the party to the court of Henry VII at Windsor, where he was subsequently established as a courtier and rose to positions of high standing, his successors becoming Dukes of Bedford.

A 17th century memorial commemorates James Napier, a fishmonger who came from Scotland and supplied fish for the ancient abbeys. From him are descended the Napier family, one of whom, Sir Robert, was made Chief Baron of the Exchequer for Ireland.

CHILCOMBE

Of unknown dedication and situated in the yard of the manor farm in a tiny churchyard comprising a few graves beneath a yew tree, this little 13th century church was partially rebuilt in the 14th century. It has neither spire nor tower, but only a small west bell turret.

Its seating capacity is 40 and it consists of a nave and chancel. There is a 12th/early 13th century font with cable moulding and a ring of arches, a Norman arch, some 15th century stained glass, and Victorian pews. In the chancel, an armchair of the Bishop family bears the carved initials, 'R.B.1642', and is thought to have stood in the same position for almost three and a half centuries. Over the chancel arch are the Creed, Lord's Prayer and Ten Commandments.

Perhaps the most interesting feature of the church is the curious panel, engraved and inlaid, which portrays scenes from the Crucifixion. Of Elizabethan date and foreign, it was used for some time as a reredos, and is believed to have been a spoil of the Armada.

 A member of the Bishop family built the adjacent manor house in 1578 and there is a memorial in the church to his great-grandson, John, whose father was MP for Bridport in the reign of Charles II. The estate later passed to Lord Nelson's family.

Like many other Dorset parishes, Chilcombe was deprived of its clergy during the Black Death.

Chilcombe

18. Towers and Spires

The primary purpose of a church tower was to house the bells, and for this purpose it needed to be substantial. Some churches have spires, many have towers. When a spire rises out of a tower, it is often known as a *steeple*. There are usually eight sides to a spire, and it may be of timber or stone according to the area where it is found. The church with its spire pointing heavenwards is a reminder that the purpose of the church is to point man to God.

Types of Spires A broach spire is one which has no parapet or low wall at its base. The square tower changes to an octagonal spire by means of corners known as *broaches*.

The *parapet spire* is more common than the broach spire and is usually of the 14th/15th century. It does not overlap the tower but rises from inside the parapet so that it is possible to walk around the base of the spire. (One would have to go to Lincolnshire to see the remarkable example at Louth, which rises to a height of 294ft).

Sometimes *timber spires* are covered with lead. (The most famous example is the crooked spire of Chesterfield Church, Derbyshire. At 229ft. this spire is said to be the tallest in the country to have been built in this way, its curious twist being the result of the lead-covered wood becoming warped over the centuries).

Terminology

LUCARNE - a dormer to a spire.

BROACH - the masonry by which the octagonal spire springs from the square tower.

CLERESTORY

Upper Hambleton - Rutland

Saxon and Norman Towers Only about eighty *Saxon towers* remain in this country and they do not have buttresses or stairways. *Norman towers* are usually low and strongly built. They are sometimes constructed in a central position on the roof of the church.

Lantern Towers In medieval times, church

towers, as well as housing the church bells, summoned folk to church and were a defence against marauders. They were known as *lantern towers* and acted as a guide to travellers by land and sea, for at night-time a beacon fire would be displayed in an iron basket, or a lamp was placed in a window in the upper storey of the tower. (Going to Lincolnshire again, a famous example is to be found at Boston in Lincolnshire. It belongs to a church dedicated to St. Botolph and known as Boston Stump - possibly because it was originally intended that a steeple should be added. From the top of the tower which is reached by 365 steps, you can see Lincoln Cathedral 32 miles away).

Detached Towers Occasionally one comes across a church with a *detached tower*. These are fairly rare in this country, and are usually only to be found where there is a lack of firm foundation – for bells when swung can exert a considerable pull on the tower they occupy.

Weather Vane (or weathercock) *Weather Vanes* exist at the top of spires or towers and are often in the form of a cock, as a reminder of the fall of St. Peter and the need for vigilance. They may represent the emblem of, say, the patron saint of the church, and sometimes they take the form of a dragon, fish, ship, violin, plough – or even an aeroplane, as at Portesham. (see chap.13)

Bell-cote (or Turret) Sometimes small churches have no tower or belfry, one bell or two being housed in an open *bell-cote (or turret)*, on the roof outside the west end of the church. These often occurred in poorer districts where it was not possible to provide anything more elaborate. A rare example exists at St. Ann, Radipole (see chap. 13) which has a triple Italianate bell turret. (See also Hermitage, chap 10.) In Saxon times, the title of 'Thane' was given to a landowner who had a church with a bell-tower on his estate.

Church Bells These played an important part in medieval times and many date from the 16th/17th centuries, some from even earlier. Most of the older bells are marked with the name of those who made them. Many churches have a ring of eight bells, the heaviest being at Sherborne Abbey (see chap.10).

Cattistock Church (see chap. 16) possesses a tall, slim tower of grey stone which at one time housed a very fine carillon of thirty-five bells. Their melodious tones were said to attract folk from far and wide until unfortunately destroyed by a fire in the tower during the war (not by enemy action).

In times past it was the custom to baptize bells, for which purpose they were 'dressed' in white 'frocks' tied with sashes. Each bell was given a sponsor (godparent), and having been sprinkled with holy water, was made to 'speak' for itself.

Bell-ringing This is an absorbing hobby, and bell-ringers are much sought after today. Bell-ringing teams go from one local church to another, ringing the bells at services and weddings and on other occasions. Rings of bells are confined almost exclusively to the Church of England.

19. Poole / Bournemouth Area

HAMPRESTON *All Saints*

Situated on the B3073 between Wimborne and West Parley, this attractive medieval dark-stoned church lies on the outer confines of Bournemouth and Poole. Its low tower dates back to the 14th century, as does the chancel, though most of the building is of later date. The north side was rebuilt in the 1890s, at which time new windows were put into the nave. Old stone floors lend atmosphere and there is a simple Norman north doorway.

Though situated near the town Hampreston village, lying close to the river Stour, possesses a scattering of cottages and farms and is pleasantly rural. Its name derives from *hame* (meadow), and the old English *preost* and *tun* (village of the priests) – possibly because the land belonged to the college of Wimborne Minster. *Hame* in the Domesday Book subsequently became in the thirteenth century *Hamme*, *Hamme Preston* and *Hamepreston*.

Parish accounts reveal that in the past, in order to keep down vermin and pests, the price of one shilling was paid for a fox, four pence for a hedgehog, and one penny for rats, while a dozen dead sparrows fetched two pence.

Somewhat strangely, a certain Henry Goldney, excommunicated from the Church of Rome, was buried at the Hampreston church in 1759.

All Saints Church, Hampreston Village

LONGFLEET *St. Mary*

This 19th century church, situated on the Longfleet Road close to Poole Hospital, has a tall spire that is a landmark for many miles around. During the 1939-45 war it was a guide to the Germans, and was found marked on the pilot's chart when an enemy plane was shot down over Poole Harbour. As the war went on, however, William Joyce (Lord Haw Haw), British broadcaster of Nazi propaganda whose aunt lived locally at Broadstone, announced that 'they were coming to bomb the little church on the hill'. Fortunately the church was not hit, though a few bombs dropped in the churchyard.

Longfleet St Mary

St Mary's interior prior to alterations

The church is by Edward Blore and dates from 1830-33; the chancel dates from 1864 and is by Street - two major exponents of Gothic architecture. This was a church built in stages, the first stage of which no longer exists. The chancel was added later, together with the tower and spire. At one time a gallery existed in the baptistry. Considerable alterations have taken place to the interior during the past fifty years.

The vicarage built in the late 1800s and pulled down in the 1960s, stood on an acre of land now covered by the extended Poole General Hospital

POOLE *St. James*

The parish church of Poole stands not far from the quay and is a fine Georgian building both inside and out. Begun in 1819, it was completed at a cost of £11,740 and consecrated in 1821. A major restoration was carried out in the 1990s. Of fine Portland stone ashlar, it is a good example of its period - a spacious, light building with a gallery on three sides supported by pillars of pitch-pine in groups of four, brought over from Newfoundland, probably on the decks of Poole brigs. The ceiling is rib-vaulted, and the masonry is faced with Purbeck limestone. There are some 18th century monuments and some very beautiful

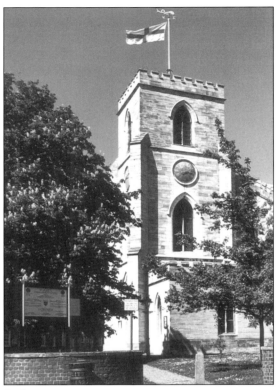

St James

stained-glass windows. The reredos, with the Creed, the Commandments and the Lord's Prayer, is good 18th century Classical. There are some charity boards in the vestibule.

A church has existed on this site since 1142 and the present building replaces one which by the early 1800s was past repairing. It was also a health hazard on account of the human remains deposited in the vault beneath.

Here in October is held the annual Service of the Sea, at which time the church is decorated with lobster pots, fishing nets suspended from pillar to pillar, and all the other equipment appropriate to the occasion.

20. Miscellaneous

Barrel Organ There are not many *Barrel Organs* remaining these days, the pipework of most having been incorporated into the traditional-type organ. Those that do exist, however, are capable of playing a number of chants and tunes (see chap. 2 Steeple).

For Organ (traditional) see chapter 7.

Chantry A *chantry* was originally a chapel endowed for the purpose of the singing of masses for the souls of the founder or others designated by him, the word being derived from the old French *'chanterie'* (*'chanter'* – to sing). This practice was discontinued at the Reformation, following the passing of the Chantry Act in 1552. (see chap. 13 Corton).

An old turret clock

Clocks There are some interesting old clocks still in existence. Mechanical clocks came into being from as early as the 12th century, though there were no clock dials until the 14th century. Even up to the 1600s village clocks were frequently without dials, the quarters, halves, three-quarters and hours being struck on bells by automatic figures of different designs called 'Jacks'. (see chap. 4 Wimborne Minster)

A Sherborne clock-maker, Thomas Bartholomew, was responsible for the *turret clocks* to be found in the churches of Yetminster, St. Andrew and Longburton, St. James (see chap. 10). Yet another old Dorset turret-clock is to be found at Puddletown, St. Mary (see chap. 16)

Clypping the Church An unusual custom takes place each year in some churches, on the Sunday following the 19th September. This is a very old tradition known as *clypping* (or *clipping*) the church and has nothing to do with clipping yew trees. Children and some adults surround the church holding hands, and are said to be 'clipping' (encircling or embracing) the church. The ceremony takes place at Upwey, St. Laurence. (see chap. 13)

Consecration Crosses At the consecration of a church, the bishop anointed twelve places inside the church and twelve places on the outside, those inside being usually marked by crosses on the walls. Occasionally one or two may still remain as, for instance, at Holnest, St. Mary where quite a number survive. (see chap. 10). Exterior ones, which would have been carved, have almost completely disappeared.

Dedications Dedications were usually in memory of a saint or an event. In order of popularity, the following dedications for old churches were: St. Mary, All Saints, St. Peter, St. Michael (a church with this dedication was often situated on a hill), St. Andrew, St. John the Baptist, and St. Nicholas. However, St. Paul and Holy Trinity were much favoured in the 19th century.

St. Laurence (or Lawrence) gives his name to a number of churches, the story connected with him being a gruesome one. When ordered to produce the treasures of the church, the silver cups and golden candlesticks, he gathered together the widows and children, the lame, the halt and the blind and presented those instead. It was for this reason that he was burnt on a massive grid set over burning coals, a replica of which can be seen at Upwey, St. Laurence (see chap.13).

For more unusual dedications see: Ryme Intrinsica, St. Hypolite (chap. 10) and Toller Fratrum, Basil the Great (see chap.16).

Liturgical Colours *Black* is worn on Good Friday and for funerals.

Green, being the colour of nature, is used throughout Epiphany and Trinity, and betokens life and hope.

Red, used at Whitsuntide (now often called Pentecost), is associated with fire and the colour of blood.

Violet, for penitence, is used in Advent and Lent.

White, representing purity and triumph, is used at Eastertide and on Trinity Sunday.

Orientation Old churches usually face from west to east with the chancel at the east end, though the reason for this is not definitely known. It is thought that it could be for one of the following reasons: because light comes from the east with the rising sun; because the Holy Land lies in that direction; or because Christ's second coming would be from the east.

Scratch Dial There are not many of these remaining. The *scratch dial* was a type of sundial used before ordinary clocks came into more common usage in the 15th century. It marked the time of church services and consisted of a dial with lines scratched into the cement-covered walls of the church. The shadow was cast by a metal rod called a 'gnomon' or 'style' which projected from a central hole from which radiated the scratched lines. Gnomons have now all disappeared, so should the church guide refer to a scratch dial on the outside south wall of the church, it may be difficult to locate. Scratch dials are always situated on south walls, the north side being sunless.

Situation The most attractive part of a small town or village is often the area surrounding the church. Some of the most interesting churches may be hidden in out-of-the-way places and take some finding – down winding country lanes, for instance, or across a field. All old churches are worth visiting, even those that originated far back in time, but have been rebuilt. Enter an old church and you will sense an atmosphere of worship – the result of constant use throughout the centuries.

Unfortunately, this book does not by any means cover all of Dorset's ancient and not so ancient ecclesiastical buildings though the chapters which deal with different aspects of medieval churches, such as porches, interiors, towers and furnishings, will enable the visitor to identify these features when they come across them in other contexts.

21. The Top Ten

As regards historical interest, architectural interest and picturesque setting.

1. STUDLAND *St. Nicholas* The best example in Dorset of a Norman church, and one of the oldest and best preserved in the country, so well worth a visit.

2. WAREHAM *St. Martin* This little church is the best example of a Saxon church in Dorset. Considerable remains of wall paintings in the chancel and over the chancel arch.

3. BERE REGIS *St. John the Baptist* This is said to be one of the loveliest churches in the country, famed for its life-size figures projecting from the roof trusses on either side of the magnificent carved and painted roof.

4. PUDDLETOWN *St. Mary* There is much of interest in this magnificent, mainly 15th century church. On entering one is struck by the fact that its seating consists entirely of box pews – with, of course, pulpit and prayer-desk combined to match!

5. SHERBORNE ABBEY *St. Mary* A fine building of Saxon origin altered by the Normans. Note the fan vaulting over the nave, and of course the Great West Window.

6. WINTERBORNE TOMSON *St. Andrew* It takes one by surprise to come upon this little redundant 12th century church, situated adjacent to a farm at the end of what at first sight appears to be a track leading nowhere!

7. WINTERBORNE ZELSTONE *St. Mary* An attractive little church in secluded small village with thatched cottages and a river running by.

8. BUCKLAND RIPERS Another charming little church in a picturesque rural setting, well worth seeking out.

9. CHALBURY *All Saints* This church has one of few Georgian interiors remaining in the county. A lovely little building, sensitively preserved.

10. MARNHULL *St. Gregory* The fine tower of this church is a landmark for miles around.